BOOKS BY

MILLARD LAMPELL

THE LONESOME TRAIN

THE LONG WAY HOME

THE HERO

JOURNEY TO THE CAPE

THE WALL

A PLAY IN TWO ACTS BY

MILLARD LAMPELL

BASED ON THE NOVEL BY

JOHN HERSEY

1961

NEW YORK : ALFRED · A · KNOPF

THE WALL

Acknowledgment is made for:
The epigraph for the Introduction, quoted from A MORAL FOR AN AGE OF PLENTY by Jacob Bronowski and published in *The Saturday Evening Post*, is used by permission of the author and *The Saturday Evening Post*.

The Introduction, "Bringing 'The Wall' to the Stage," by Millard Lampell, originally appeared in the Autumn 1960 issue of *Midstream*.

The lyrics for "Shpunt's Song" by Millard Lampell and Robert De Cormier and for "Sky Is Free" (Song of the Beggar Children) by Millard Lampell and Robert De Cormier, Copyright © MCMLX by Leeds Music Corporation, New York, N.Y., are used by permission.

The illustrations in this volume are reproduced from photographs by Werner J. Kuhn.

L. C. catalog card number: 61–9233

 Manufactured in the United States of America. Published simultaneously in Canada by McClelland & Stewart, Ltd.

FIRST EDITION

FOR

ZIVIA AND ANTEK

INTRODUCTION

"There are two things that make up morality. One is the sense that other people matter: the sense of common loyalty, of charity and tenderness, the sense of human love. The other is a clear judgment of what is at stake: a cold knowledge, without a trace of deception, of precisely what will happen to oneself and to others if one plays either the hero or the coward." J. BRONOWSKI

It was sometime early in the winter of 1958, when I began to explore the possibility of writing a play based upon John Hersey's novel, *The Wall.*

I had read the book when it first appeared in 1950, and found it a shattering and strangely tender work. Yet I approached the prospect of turning it into a play with considerable doubt. The Nazi extermination of the Jews of Warsaw and the Ghetto revolt seemed a highly unlikely subject for Broadway.

One did not have to be an expert to know that what the postwar American theatrical audience craved above all was a bright, bouncy musical. And in straight plays, what they flocked to see was sex, sophisticated comedy, and sentimentality. A savage seduction, a fusillade of wisecracks, or a good cry with an upbeat ending.

As for the important plays of the decade, more and more they had come to focus on the themes of isolation and defeat. The best of them were brilliant character portraits, miniatures painted in terrifying detail: lonely souls in a twilight landscape, crying agonizedly into the deaf wind. All their voices seemed to echo in the words of Val, in Tennessee Williams's *Orpheus Descending:*

"Nobody ever gets to know *no body!* We're all sentenced to solitary confinement within our own skins for life!"

How many nights have I sat in a theater, watching a painful interplay of blind victims groping along as they waited for fate to crush them.

I have seen fascinating and talented plays in which the dimensions of the world were no more than the size of a bed. Plays in which nothing existed beyond the walls of the set. Plays in which the social forces acting upon the characters were enigmatic and bewildering, like signposts in a fog.

Man as a helpless victim. I do not deny that this is a truth of our time. But it is only one truth. There are others. There is understanding, and indomitable faith, and the rare, exultant moment when one human finally reaches out to accept another.

I am not talking about false romanticism. I am talking of men as we know them—greedy, frightened, foolish, contradictory, uncertain, despairing, and yet in spite of it all, stumbling toward a possible dignity.

I believe that the world shapes man—and also that man can shape the world. People can learn and grow, and they can consciously decide to act, for good or evil. People can submit—and they can also resist.

Whether writing of Europe in 1940, or America in 1960, I should be compelled to seek out some facet of that theme.

And so, whatever the theatrical odds against it, I found myself drawn to the story of the Warsaw Ghetto. For if ever there were people who should have been helpless and paralyzed, the Jews of Nazi-occupied Warsaw were those people. Yet, undeniably, six hundred of them searched out the secret truth of what was happening around them, and facing their fate without illusion, they trusted each other, organized, and passionately resisted.

As I write this, barely a month after the Broadway opening, the Habima Theatre is already in rehearsal for its production of *The Wall* in Israel. Other productions are being prepared in Germany, England, and Poland, and negotiations are under way with Holland, South Africa, Sweden, and Italy. Clearly there seems to be room on the stages of the world for plays that concern themselves with man's conscious struggle to keep from drowning in the swirl of events.

And yet, *The Wall* as a drama came within a hairsbreadth of not being born.

To begin with, I had never written a play before. And if ever a novel was designed to scare even the most battle-scarred playwright, *The Wall* was it. The book is a vast tapestry running more than six hundred pages. It covers a span of almost four turbulent years, shifts scene to a hundred locales, introduces more than fifty important characters, and invokes several of the most crucial moral issues of our time. It was as though one had decided to try one's hand at sculpturing, and chose the Himalayas for a first chunk of stone.

One serious doubt concerned the matter of working with someone else's material. I had, before then, written cantatas, poems, and a number of books and films. Good or bad, every word of them had sprung out of my own emotions.

To simply transfer intact a small bit of *The Wall* to the stage would not have interested me as a writer, and would have done bitter violence to the novel. The story of the Warsaw Ghetto was inextricably woven across an arc of time. To attempt to cram it into a day, a week, would be to distort it completely. Also, a major character of the event was the Ghetto itself—that raucous, teeming, funny, tragic, furiously alive community beating like surf against its prison wall. To try to compress it within a single room would cripple what was profoundly significant: the *size* of what took place.

I hadn't the foggiest notion of how I would approach the form of the play, but I knew that I had to be free to experiment, try anything, change, transform, create as I chose. A play is an intricate mechanism and has its own inner logic. I remember William Gibson warning me: "A novel is like taking a walk. You can explore side alleys, stop to think, double back. But a play is like a plane ride. If you stop before your destination, you're dead."

This dilemma was solved very simply by Hersey himself. Once he decided that we shared the same point of view about life, he offered the freedom to work as I chose, supporting it with a decision not to read the manuscript or see the play until opening night.

I began by rereading the book twice. I was shaken by the immensity of the events it portrayed. It was small consolation that I need not hew to the story, scene by scene. I was responsible for trying to capture its spirit. And beyond that, as Hersey had been, I was responsible to the people who had played out that terrible hour in history.

I turned back to the documents and records. Perhaps no crucial time was ever so painstakingly recorded by its participants. The Jews of Warsaw seem to have been obsessed by the thought that they might be wiped off the face of the earth, and no one would ever know how it happened. And the truth is that while it was going on, the world did not know. Checking back, I discovered that even during the final days of resistance, only a fragile echo filtered outside the wall: a few words over the London radio, a line or two buried in the back pages of one, *exactly one,* New York newspaper.

But the Jews of Warsaw had left behind them an immense cache of diaries, letters, notes. After the war, bit by bit, these began to come to light from under the stones of prison cells, from hiding places beneath the charred ruins. There were the monumental, incredibly detailed archives of the historian Emmanuel Ringelblum, dug up in their sealed, rubberized milk cans. They contained everything from Ghetto newspapers and concert programs to collections of jokes going the rounds, simple yet haunting statistics, and private ironies (the code name for Hitler was Horowitz).

And not least of all, there were the meticulous records of the Germans. Military correspondence, orders of the day, laws and regulations. It was the files of the Nazi commandant charged with leveling the Ghetto, SS General Stroop, that provided the most detailed portrait of the Jewish resistance. This same Stroop had his teams of combat photographers prepare an elaborate volume of pictures of the battle of the Ghetto.

For months I pored over these diaries and documents, children's poems, mementoes, stained snapshots rescued from God knows what piles of clothing.

History has its own peculiar eyesight. It concerns itself with what is unique. And what was unique in Warsaw was the scope of man's inhumanity to man. So mostly the familiar details of ordinary life were passed over in the desperate haste of setting down the story of annihilation. I finished my research with an overwhelming sense of ashes and agony.

At this point, I was almost persuaded to drop

the project. I am a writer chiefly concerned with life, not death. And that was what I simply lost track of in the ruins: amid all the tragic mementoes, the wreckage of the destroyed Ghetto, I simply could not recognize human life as I knew it.

My original purpose in writing the play was to write something more than the story of Warsaw's Jewry. For this was a moment in history when the Jews of Warsaw spoke for all mankind. I had no desire to romanticize them, or to do any special pleading. I simply wished to present them as I believe they were—tragic, jealous, warm, frightened, tormented, cruel, courageous—in short, a mirror of the human race with all its failings and all its astonishing potential.

A number of questions haunted me. Of the more than half a million Jews in Warsaw, no more than six hundred actually joined the resistance. Why did so few fight, and why did they wait so long to take up arms? What was the significance of the bitter role played by the Jewish police and the Jewish Gestapo informers? And finally, the universal question—perhaps *the* question of our time—under what conditions does man abandon his individual drive for self-protection, and commit himself to his fellow man?

I knew that I could only find the answers by crossing to the other side of the wall, and settling down to live within the Ghetto; by attempting to experience life as it was lived in Warsaw, 1940.

There is no today that is not shaped by yesterdays. I was born in New Jersey, of Austrian immigrant stock. I had never been in Poland, and knew virtually nothing of the culture and traditions of Warsaw Jewry. And so I plunged into that vast, rich sea, reading Peretz and Sholem Aleichem, Mendele Mocher Seforim, collections of Yiddish proverbs, folk tales, and songs, and all that I could find of the modern writers of Vilna, Bialystok, Lublin, and Warsaw. A year before, I had been barely familiar with three or four Yiddish and Hebrew writers. Now I delved into the work of Sutzkever and Katznelson, the poet laureate of the Jewish resistance.

It was at this point that someone called to tell me that a former commander of the Ghetto Fighters Organization was in New York for a brief visit. His name was Yitzchak Zukerman; his underground name had been Captain Antek.

Late the next afternoon, I found myself outside a room in a hotel on the West Side. I knocked, and the door was opened by a tall, shaggy man with a blond mustache and blue eyes. Antek.

We struggled through introductions in broken bits of three languages. He was polite but guarded. Clearly he had had some uncomfortable experiences with writers seeking a fairytale of glory. Hersey's book served as preliminary credentials. But Antek had to find out for himself who I was, and what I was really after.

Slowly, through the following weeks, he probed, questioned, watched me with those blue, appraising eyes. Bit by bit, the door between us opened on friendship. He came home to meet my family, to wiggle his ears for my enchanted daughter, to pull out a fistful of photographs of his own two sturdy, sunburned children and his small, indomitable wife, Zivia, who had led a fighting group in the Ghetto.

"Yes, the women were the strongest. It is not a pleasant thing for men to admit, but it is so. Women are realistic, they must learn to live with the simple details of life, to adjust, to prepare for the worst. Sometimes a sudden wind can crack a cedar, but the grass bends and survives. The women were like grass." Antek grinned. "You can see that I love women."

He was so full of life. His laugh was huge, and his talk could turn from Tolstoy to the grape harvest, from the morning news to the psalms of David.

Once, speaking of the resistance, I remember him saying: "If you look back at the height of the fighting, what we did seems incredible. But you must remember that it was a process. It took years to develop." His eyes twinkled. "We were young, remember. We were prepared, we had an idea, and we were very young. I was twenty-three. A wonderful age to do stupid things."

And another night, as we sat around listening to an old record of Bessie Smith singing the blues, Antek abruptly leaned forward and asked me: "Would you believe that in the worst days, when everything was burning, when we were hiding away in the bunkers, we drank and laughed, argued and sang, kissed in the shadows? You must know that, if you wish to write about the Ghetto."

After the weeks we spent together, whenever I thought of the Warsaw Ghetto, I thought first of Antek. Warsaw was a far cry from the meek, introspective world of Sholem Aleichem's towns. These were not quaint, mystical people. They were tough, resilient, independent, energetic. An outgoing and passionate community—curious, restless, sharp, and vocal. There was a tenement peevishness and a tenement exuberance. A life painted in bold colors. A life mirrored perfectly in their humor. Their wry, sardonic, bitter-sweet mockery of themselves. They did not tell jokes just to be funny. It was also a way of putting the harsh reality of their lives into a shape that was easier to deal with.

And there was something that bound them all together. A folk memory, a culture, a common historical experience. However much they rebelled against it, history had made them a family. And this tended to heighten emotions and relationships, to give them a certain swift recognition of each other's characters, a sensitivity to subtle shifts of mood. They struggled against the ties, but they were inescapably bound to each other.

A family. With a family's feuds and hatreds, and a family's fierce loyalties. Perhaps from this it is possible to understand how they could have perpetrated upon each other the most savage cruelties and also the most tender love. They reflected all mankind, a little larger than life.

Later I was to meet two other Ghetto fighters. One was a woman named Chana Fryshdorf, and one was Antek's wife, Zivia—three of the fourteen still alive—all that is left of the six hundred Jews who stood off a German army with a few pistols and some bottles of gasoline.

In one way, all three survivors were the same. They were brimmingly, marvelously alive.

Half a million Warsaw Jews were exterminated. And yet my sharpest image of the Ghetto became one not of death, but of stubborn life. The grim, anonymous figures in the ashes vanished. I saw Antek, Zivia, Chana—myself, my family, my friends—actual and ordinary people who laughed, squabbled, fell in love, were terrified, tender, ridiculous.

With all this inside me, I began to shape the characters for the play, and to place inside them the spirit of the Ghetto and its philosophical questions.

In drawing Rachel, I held close to Hersey's strong, plain "little mother," a fully committed woman who was capable of giving faith and love to those around her.

With Berson, I chose to reflect something that was perhaps only a shadow in Hersey's character: a defensive wariness of committing himself. My Berson became two men, one of them crouched and hiding inside the other. His first article of faith is personal survival. It is only in crisis, when Berson is forced to act swiftly, that something else flashes to the surface, a realization of his need of others. This shakes him, he feels he cannot live up to the responsibility, and so he flees the Ghetto. But his flight is already too late. His identity already depends on others—chiefly Rachel. When he finally returns to the Ghetto, in the midst of the fighting, he explains: "I always thought that just to live was enough. To live *how?* To live *with whom?*"

Into the character of Shpunt, the peddler, I poured elements from a number of Hersey's characters, plus a taste of my mother's relentless, shrewd pessimism. All his life, Shpunt has been a cart-horse, sweating for his daily bread. He is a living embodiment of folk experience, the Eternal

Jew, hungry, leathery, determined to survive, whatever the cost. All his life he has been at the beck and call of others, which is what makes him so touchy. He is canny, overworked, realistic, a poor man, who cannot afford the luxury of idealizing life. He loves to haggle and argue, but he has none of the icy emotions: cruelty, malice, calculated hatred. He has the spontaneous irritation of a man who since childhood has always been forced to carry something heavy. The actual crates, bundles, packages, and chairs are symbols of an eternal load: being a Jew in the world of Poland.

He has an instinctive, furious loyalty, not to individuals or even to God, but to a heritage of endurance. He is like an alley-cat—however violently you fling him down, he will land on his feet.

He is dour and pessimistic because he has learned that if one prepares for the worst, one will be ready for whatever comes. His gruff complaints conceal a grudging love for any Jew who resists.

Endurance, endurance. Shpunt admires, above all, endurance. And he himself will endure, as a folk tale endures, misshapen by being handed down and pushed around, all sharp edges and queer corners, but defiantly and unashamedly thrusting his face at the world and hooting his bitter complaints.

But he is also, remember, the grandson of Hassidim, a poetic, ecstatic sect. And so there is something light and gay in his singing and dancing. A sort of Sabbath face that pops out now and then. For as the Hassidim said: "The Jewish people are an enchanted prince who has been turned into a dog, and leads a dog's life on week days, but reverts to his joyous self on the Sabbath."

The thread that bound all my characters and provided the chief dramatic suspense of the play was a question. How long will it take them to believe that the Nazis mean to exterminate them? And a twin question. When they believe they are marked to die, will they resist?

I remember sitting in Central Park one sunny winter afternoon with one of the few surviving Ghetto fighters. She suddenly turned to me, and in a tormented voice said softly: "This will be an eternal mystery—why didn't we resist when they began to resettle us?" (I was later to place these exact words in the mouth of Rachel.)

A volume might be written on these two questions. Certainly the population of the Warsaw Ghetto did not believe the first reports of the gas chambers. The first man to escape from a death train and return with a description of Treblinka became a pariah in the Ghetto. His friends shunned him; he was refused work, branded as a lunatic.

In the early days, I am convinced, the refusal to believe the Nazi policy of annihilation was rooted in a life wish. Man wishes to survive, and so he discounts the possibility of imminent death. He thinks: something will happen, I will be saved somehow. And another powerful human characteristic was at work: resistance to change. The desire to continue life as usual, to find comfort in the familiar. To accept the gas chambers as a reality meant, if Warsaw's Jews were to follow any logic, completely changing one's way of life. Joining the resistance meant moving out of one's apartment, going into hiding, training one's self to kill, and to die if necessary.

Resistance is a process, as Antek said. Those who fought in the Warsaw Ghetto were mostly those who were already members of illegal organizations. In the later days, there were many young people who finally understood what was happening, and wanted to join the resistance. But by then it was too late. There were simply no arms, food, or hiding places for them.

The main body of the Jewish Fighters Organization was composed of those who, from their early years on, had been joiners. Zionists, Socialists, members of political groups tinged with every color of the rainbow. They were not "loners," each making his isolated way. They were the committed. Their faith in man was stronger than their awe of machines. They had learned, back in the thirties, the power of a dedicated and skilled bare hand.

From a study of the documents, one gains a sick respect for the psychological insight of the Nazis. They understood the human will to survive, and the delusions that can spring from it. With every pound of death, they portioned out a teaspoonful of hope. The placards announcing deportations always started by listing those who were to be exempt. Forged postcards were sent back from the imaginary "factories on the Eastern front" announcing to friends and relatives that the deportees were safe and happy.

And the Nazis also understood the numbing and demoralizing impact of surprise. They were forever establishing certain routines, and then suddenly changing them for no reason. One day only women were taken for deportation. The next day, only children. One month the house raids ended at twilight. The next month they suddenly began to occur at night. The Germans carefully exploited the terror of the unexpected. They also used the terror of abrupt, senseless violence. Quite early in the occupation days there were incidents of meaningless slaughter. These were deliberately calculated to unnerve the Jewish population. And they had their effect.

As much of this as I could, I sought to capture in my play. It explains a good deal of why the Jews took so long to organize resistance.

Yet, at long last, resistance there was. And more than just Warsaw. Resistance in Lublin, resistance even in the crematorium of Treblinka.

Out of all the horror of Hitler Europe, it is this that to me emerged as the most significant fact. A handful of Jews exposed the fullest potential of the human race. To resist death. To trust one another. To commit themselves. To endure.

And so this became virtually the final speech of my play: Rachel praying that she is pregnant, and answering Berson's doubts about the future with: ". . . the only way to answer death is with more life."

M. L.

THE WALL

was produced by *Kermit Bloomgarden* and *Billy Rose*

AT THE

BILLY ROSE THEATRE

New York City, on the night of October 11, 1960
with the following in the Cast:

PAVEL MENKES . . . . *Vincent Gardenia*
FISHEL SHPUNT . . . . *Joseph Buloff*
DOLEK BERSON . . . . *George C. Scott*
GERMAN PRIVATE . . . . *James Nielsen*
KATZ . . . . *James Ray*
REB MAZUR . . . . *Muni Seroff*
HALINKA APT . . . . *Claudette Nevins*
RACHEL APT . . . . *Yvonne Mitchell*
SYMKA BERSON . . . . *Marian Seldes*
MORDECAI APT . . . . *Michael Ebert*
PAN APT . . . . *David Opatoschu*
DAVID APT . . . . *Paul Mace*
STEFAN MAZUR . . . . *Robert Drivas*
RUTKA MAZUR . . . . *Leila Martin*
RAPPAPORT . . . . *Leon B. Stevens*
SLONIM . . . . *Sol Frieder*

Directed by MORTON DA COSTA
Settings and Lighting by HOWARD BAY
Costumes by NOEL TAYLOR
Musical Supervision by ROBERT DE CORMIER

SYNOPSIS OF SCENES

The action of the play covers the period
from the spring of 1940 to the spring of 1943
—on a street in Warsaw

ACT I

SCENE 1 · The street. Spring 1940.
SCENE 2 · The Apt apartment. Several hours later.
SCENE 3 · The street. Six months later.
SCENE 4 · The street. The following spring.
SCENE 5 · The Apt apartment. The following winter.
SCENE 6 · The Apt apartment. A week later.

ACT II

SCENE 1 · The street. Summer 1942.
SCENE 2 · The Apt apartment. Two weeks later.
SCENE 3 · The street. Several days later.
SCENE 4 · The bakery. The following day.
SCENE 5 · The street. Spring 1943.
SCENE 6 · An underground bunker. Almost three weeks later.

CHARACTERS

<table>
<tr><td>DOLEK BERSON
SYMKA, his wife
RACHEL APT
HALINKA, her sister
DAVID, their brother, age 9
MORDECAI, their older brother
PAN APT, their father
REB MAZUR (a rabbi)
STEFAN, his son
RUTKA, his daughter</td><td>Residents of the house</td></tr>
</table>

PAVEL MENKES (*a baker*)
FISHEL SHPUNT (*a peddler*)
CLERK
PAN KOGAN
PANI KOGAN
REGINA, *their daughter*

O. S. FUEHRER
GERMAN SERGEANT
GERMAN PRIVATE

<table>
<tr><td>RAPPAPORT
SLONIM
KATZ</td><td>Members of the underground</td></tr>
</table>

WOMAN IN A BABUSHKA

JEWS OF THE GHETTO

ACT I

« »

(The key to the sets is simplicity, almost an abstraction of place. The Ghetto was a crisscrossed, teeming world. Life eddied restlessly from the streets into the houses and back again. It is this atmosphere, this constant flow that is important. Settings are described realistically only because true style must be woven out of reality.)

(The events of the play cover a span of three years. Where there is a passage of time between scenes, it is carried by music or sound. The Ghetto was never silent. In time, its people developed the acute hearing of the blind. They listened anxiously, as sailors scan a sky for signs. In the echo of a laugh, a scream, a shot, an ax blow, voices complaining or singing, they caught the portents of danger, defiance, and even desperate hope.)

SHPUNT: And don't blink your eyes at me. I'm not buying any coat racks!

ACT I: *Scene 1*

SERGEANT: Out. Everybody out.

ACT I: *Scene 3*

[SCENE 1]

A street in Warsaw. A district of worn buildings hung with cast-iron balconies.

The street runs parallel with the footlights. At center, an alley climbs a flight of steps leading away upstage. At left, stands a bakery. At right, is an apartment house that is on its way to becoming a tenement.

It is a bright spring afternoon. Sunlight slants innocently among the branches of a linden tree —a frail touch of green in a stone world.

Parked in front of the house is a handcart piled with furniture and a jumble of household odds and ends.

PAVEL MENKES *comes down from his shop to inspect the cart. He is a baker, a huge man, practical as bread.*

Down the steps, center, an ornate chair enters. A pair of staggering human legs leads to a suspicion that buried somewhere beneath it is a man.

As the chair approaches the cart, MENKES *moves to intercept it.*

MENKES: What have you got there? [*Catching hold of the chair*] Let me see.

VOICE [*muffled*]: Let go!

MENKES: Look at that tapestry. It must have cost a fortune.

[*The chair sways, trying to pull free.*]

VOICE: Get your hands off!

MENKES: That's a genuine antique you've got there. [*As the chair jerks away violently*] Look out!

[*The chair teeters and falls with a crash, revealing a scowling gnome*—FISHEL SHPUNT.

SHPUNT'S *face has a magnificent ugliness. It is more than a face; it is a mask of tragedy, giving a certain grandeur to this little man in a battered coat.* SHPUNT *regards life with habitual suspicion and fury, as though it were an old enemy forever trying to swindle him.*]

SHPUNT: I told you to let go.

MENKES [*picking up the chair*]: Shaa, it's all right. Nothing's damaged.

SHPUNT: The gilt is chipped.

MENKES: It's not chipped. [*Sitting experimentally*] A regular throne, eh? A pleasure.

SHPUNT: Maybe you'd like to buy it.

MENKES: I'm a baker, not an aristocrat.

SHPUNT: So, up, up, you're sagging in the springs. [*As* MENKES *rises heavily*] I'll let you have a bargain. I'm not a well man. Make me an offer —I'll use it to pay for my funeral.

MENKES: Every time I see you, you're on your last legs.

SHPUNT [*catching* MENKES's *hand and pressing it to his chest*]: Feel. You feel? Palpitations.

MENKES: You've been on your last legs for eighteen years.

SHPUNT: It's a miracle I'm still standing here. Last night, just as I was getting up from the table, I began to get hot and cold flashes. Shooting pains in the head, my heart jumping like a fish. I said to myself: "Fishel, this is the end." I saw the Angel of Death, he had green eyes and was eating a bunch of grapes. He crooked his finger at me and made a sound, tck, tck, like you call a horse. I fell on the floor, everything went black . . .

MENKES: And?

SHPUNT: I heard a clock strike. I said to myself: "In heaven who needs clocks?" So I decided I was still alive. I got up and made myself a glass of tea.

MENKES: Shpunt, Shpunt, you'll outlive us all.

SHPUNT: From your mouth to God's ears. [*Coughs*] You hear? Hitler should have what I've got in my chest. I give myself another week.

[DOLEK BERSON *enters. He is in his early thirties, lithe and somehow boyish. There is a gusto about him, an appetite for life. He has an avid curiosity and a quick laugh—perhaps too quick. A charming drifter who has used all his resources to avoid coming to grips with life.*]

MENKES: Hello, Dolek. You're just in time for Shpunt's funeral.

BERSON: He died again?

MENKES: Last night.

BERSON [*regarding* SHPUNT *critically*]: He looks nice, the way they laid him out. Better than when he was alive.

SHPUNT: Go ahead, make a joke. [*Sets chair on cart.*] Hitler, may a black plague fall on him, picks up Poland and cracks it like a walnut. Houses blown to bits, fifty thousand killed. So go ahead, make jokes.

BERSON: The Germans have been here for six months, they haven't laid a hand on you.

SHPUNT: In Radom they burned down a synagogue.

BERSON: Stop groaning, Shpunt. Look at the sky. It's April, a beautiful day.

SHPUNT [*exiting into house*]: On beautiful days they also bury people.

MENKES: So, Dolek, did you find a job?

BERSON: Just when you think winter is going to last forever, you wake up one morning and the birds are singing.

MENKES: You didn't find a job.

BERSON: I went for a walk. Looked at the women strolling down Marshalkovska Street. It's amazing what a fine day can do. Even the whores look respectable. I'm not sure it's an improvement. [*Inspecting linden tree*] Look at those new leaves—that green.

MENKES [*starts toward bakery, then turns*]: I've known you for twenty-five years: you haven't changed. You are a boy, Berson, that's your trouble. You are not a responsible man.

BERSON [*amiably*]: Also, I'm lazy. [*Spying chair in cart*] Elegant. Where did he get it?

MENKES [*drawn back*]: From your new neighbors. The family that moved in across the hall last week.

BERSON [*takes down chair*]: Name is Apt. Owns a jewelry store.

MENKES: So why do they want to move in here?

BERSON: They had a fancy apartment on the river, the Germans requisitioned it.

MENKES: They're beginning already. Grabbing. [*Turns to go*]

BERSON: I haven't really been around the city since the siege ended. They've started up the merry-go-round again in Krasinski Park. There's an old man outside the Bristol Hotel selling pussy willows. Where does he find pussy willows?

MENKES: I saw your wife this morning. She stopped in for a dozen rolls.

BERSON: Oh, my God, Symka. Today is our anniversary. I meant to buy her a present. Fifth anniversary . . . something wooden. Maybe Shpunt's got something.

MENKES: Berson, do yourself a favor. Get yourself a job and settle down. [BERSON *is rummaging in the cart.*] I hear over at Mundlak's hardware store they're looking for a locksmith.

[SHPUNT *has entered, carrying a mirror.*]

SHPUNT [*noticing chair*]: How did that get off the cart? Put it back.

BERSON: Gently.

SHPUNT: Look at him! Loafs all day, and he's got shoulders like an ox. And me with my gallstones, I have to work like a . . .

BERSON: Relax, Fishel. You can always hang yourself later.

[*They stiffen as a German* PRIVATE *enters. He is a callow, handsome boy of nineteen.*]

PRIVATE [*to* BERSON]: Pardon me. Could you tell me the way to the Jewish Community Council building?

BERSON: Straight ahead one block, and turn left.

PRIVATE: Thank you. [*He exits.*]

BERSON: Handsome boys, eh? A nation of football players. Hear that voice? You could have baked a cake with it.

MENKES: You look Polish, so he was polite. [*Starting toward bakery*] Go around to Mundlak's, Dolek, before they close.

BERSON [*rummaging in cart*]: Yes, I'll go, I'll go.

MENKES: Go.

BERSON: I'll go! [MENKES *exits into bakery. From the depths of the cart,* BERSON *brings up a concertina.*] Look at this little sweetheart. Where did you get it?

SHPUNT: Picked it up this morning, over in Mila Street.

[KATZ *has entered. A wiry, intense young man. He wears a torn sheepskin coat.*]

KATZ: Did you see him? That German bastard? That's him, that's the one.

BERSON: What one?

KATZ: I've been following him for half an hour. He threw a girl off a moving streetcar.

BERSON: What did she do?

KATZ: Looked at him crosseyed. Sneezed. How do I know what she did? Come on.

BERSON: Where?

KATZ: After him.

BERSON: Sure. Go grab a pumpernickel, run and hit him over the head.

KATZ: We'll catch him in a back alley.

BERSON: Katz, don't be preposterous.

KATZ: An eye for an eye.

BERSON: It's not just one soldier, Katz. Get it through your head. It's an army. Only five days it took them to wipe out Holland, Belgium, Norway . . .

SHPUNT: They've got us, like mice in a cage. Wait. We'll suffer.

KATZ: Who's asking you?

SHPUNT: Suffer. Because we didn't obey the eleventh commandment. "Thou shalt convert thy grandfather and grandmother."

KATZ [*to* BERSON]: You coming? Yes or no?

BERSON: Bend with the wind, Katz. You try to stand up, they'll break your bones.

KATZ: They'll spit in your eye, and what? You'll pretend it's raining? [*He hurries off.*]

BERSON: A dangerous boy. [*Waving the concertina*] So—how much?

SHPUNT: What do you need with it? Better take a nice chair.

BERSON: A chair? What can you do with a chair except sit in it?

SHPUNT: And with that box?

BERSON: Ah . . . hidden away in this little box are the songs of childhood. . . . [*Starts to play* "Dort'n, Dort'n."] The first time you fell in love . . . Chopin . . . Bach . . .

SHPUNT: So for Bach, all right, give me twenty-five zlotys.

[REB MAZUR *enters—bearded, breathless, bursting with news.*]

REB MAZUR: *Sholem aleichem,* my friends. Listen—

BERSON: *Aleichem sholem.* [*To* SHPUNT] How much?

SHPUNT: Why should we argue? Give me twenty zlotys.

BERSON: I can't afford it.

REB MAZUR: Listen, I just came from the house of study—

SHPUNT [*to* BERSON]: That's real mother-of-pearl, those keys. Give me eighteen zlotys and take it.

BERSON [*reluctantly puts concertina back on cart*]: What I really need is something for Symka.

REB MAZUR: You should wear a coat, Dolek, you'll

catch pneumonia. Listen—news. The Germans have forbidden us to gather for prayer.

SHPUNT: Ah-hah, what did I tell you? It's starting.

REB MAZUR: A new law this morning. Absolutely forbidden. They came to the house of study, put up a paper.

SHPUNT: Ah-hah. They're getting down to business.

REB MAZUR: Still, only this morning I heard . . . on absolute authority, the Germans will be out of Warsaw by June. All right. So. The main thing is to have faith.

SHPUNT [*addressing an imaginary listener*]: You hear? Have faith. Hoo-hah. [*Bitterly, to his imaginary friend*] He says two hundred prayers a day. A prayer when he eats an apple, a prayer when he buttons his pants—

BERSON: Is that a way to talk to a rabbi?

SHPUNT: He can afford to have faith. When it comes to heaven he's got connections.

BERSON: Enough.

REB MAZUR: Naa, naa. I'm not offended. Leave him alone. He's not a well man.

SHPUNT: Don't apologize for me!

REB MAZUR: The way I look at it, there's nothing to worry about. Trouble we'll have—plenty. But as for anything worse, the Germans wouldn't dare. World opinion wouldn't stand for it. England, America . . . [*starts toward bakery.*]

SHPUNT: All right, I'll wait for world opinion. And while I'm waiting, I'll jump out of a window.

REB MAZUR [*entering bakery*]: Menkes, you hear? They passed a law against holding prayer services. . . .

[HALINKA APT *appears from the house. She is twenty, but appears younger. A slim beauty with blonde hair and fresh skin. She carries herself like a child who is secretly pretending to be a princess.*]

HALINKA: Pan Shpunt! You didn't by any chance take a mirror? [*She spies it on the cart.*] There, that one, with the cherry-wood frame.

BERSON: Hello, Panna Apt.

HALINKA: Hello. [*to* SHPUNT] I'm afraid there has been a mistake. The mirror wasn't to go.

SHPUNT: Your sister said—

HALINKA: My sister made a mistake. We're not selling it. [*Disarming*] I'm sorry. It's very precious to me. A birthday present from my father.

BERSON: All settled in the new apartment?

HALINKA: Settled? We haven't begun. Boxes everywhere—it looks like a railway station. The wallpaper is peeling in the living room, and at night the plumbing makes noises.

BERSON: Pitah-poom! Faa! Faa! Brrm!

HALINKA [*delightedly*]: Oh, yes, that's it. Exactly.

BERSON: We've got the only toilets in Warsaw that can play Wagner.

HALINKA: Is that you I hear in the evenings, at the piano?

BERSON: A nuisance?

HALINKA: Oh no, I love it.

BERSON: You play?

HALINKA: I sing a little. American songs, I learned them from the films. I've got an uncle in Cincinnati, America. Isn't that a marvelous name? Cincinnati.

SHPUNT [*approaches*]: So what do we do about the mirror? I counted it in when I figured the price.

HALINKA: Come inside and I'll give you something else for it. There's a nice coat rack.

SHPUNT: A coat rack? I need a coat rack like I need a broken leg.

HALINKA: Then something else.

SHPUNT [*taking mirror*]: Run inside, run outside.

HALINKA: Please!

SHPUNT: And don't blink your eyes at me. I'm not buying any coat racks! [*He exits.*]

HALINKA: Why is he so cross? It makes me nervous.

BERSON: I'll come later, and help with the boxes.

HALINKA [*an enchanting smile*]: Thank you. [*She exits.*]

[BERSON *stands looking after her, as* REB MAZUR *enters and crosses to him.*]

BERSON: That face, eh? Aie, is that a face. You wouldn't think such a look of innocence could still exist in this world.

REB MAZUR: Dolek, you're a married man, Dolek.

BERSON: I'm appreciating. Just because I look at a bird, doesn't mean I have to go hunting.

REB MAZUR [*sitting in chair*]: You saw the other sister?

BERSON: She's no bargain. But this Halinka. With that face. It could melt steel.

[*Enter* SHPUNT *carrying coat rack.*]

SHPUNT [*ironically, to* REB MAZUR]: Go ahead, make yourself comfortable. Sit, sit, I'll bring you a chicken. [REB MAZUR *rises, and* SHPUNT *takes the chair*]

REB MAZUR [*to* BERSON]: You coming in?

BERSON: I have to find a present for my wife.

REB MAZUR: So. *Shalom,* Fishel. [*He exits into the house.*]

BERSON: Maybe you've got some nice little thing. Wooden. An inlaid box, maybe . . . [*He takes up the concertina.*]

SHPUNT: Give me fifteen zlotys, take it and run, before I change my mind. [*He turns away, his open palm stretched back.*] I'll close my eyes, I shouldn't see you practically stealing.

BERSON [*laughs*]: All right, all right, you win. [*As*

he is paying SHPUNT, *the* CLERK *enters from left.*]

CLERK: I'm from the Community Council. Come, we need you. Hurry. [*Muttering to himself*] Two, four, eight, and two makes ten. Six more, when in God's name am I going to find six more? Come on, quick, quick!

BERSON: Sorry. I'm busy.

CLERK [*unheeding, turns to* SHPUNT]: Stand up straight, let me see. [*Yanking at* SHPUNT'S *coat*] Aie! Haven't you got a tie? Stand up, you look like you're dying.

SHPUNT [*knocks away* CLERK'S *hands*]: If I'm dying, that's my business!

CLERK: What do they expect me to pick up in the streets, prime ministers? Let's go.

SHPUNT: Go where?

CLERK: The Council—

SHPUNT: Are you crazy? I'll go away––who is going to watch my cart?

CLERK: The Germans have called a meeting. They gave us fifteen minutes to round up the councilors. We're taking anybody we can get.

BERSON: I am deeply honored—

CLERK: Come!

BERSON: —but I've got an important errand to do.

CLERK: This comes first.

BERSON: Find somebody else. I, ah . . . [*Improvising*] It's my grandmother's birthday.

CLERK [*drops his confused, frantic air, and stares at* BERSON. *Then quietly*]: I would appreciate your coming immediately.

BERSON: Leave me out of this. It has nothing to do with me.

CLERK: Yes, it has to do with you . . . and your wife, and all your relatives, including your sixteenth cousin.

BERSON: Look at us, do we look like councilors? It isn't logical.

[*From left, the German* PRIVATE *enters, looks at his watch, and stands waiting.*]

CLERK [*low and bitter*]: What world are you living in, my friend? This is a conquered city. What gave you the idea there is any question of logic?

[*Now they all become aware of the German* PRIVATE, *who looks at his watch again.*]

PRIVATE [*calmly*]: Three minutes.

CLERK: I think you had better come.

[CLERK *turns and starts out, knowing that they will follow. And they do.*]

[*Lights dim out on the scene.*]

[*Off, the merry-go-round is heard playing in the park. It fades as the scene changes.*]

[SCENE 2]

The living room of the APT *flat.*

Expensive furniture in disarray. Half-emptied crates, piles of books, and dishes. A door, right, leads off to the bedroom. Another doorway, upstage, leads back to the kitchen. A third door, left, leads out to the hallway.

RACHEL *enters from the kitchen, carrying a framed picture and a small suitcase.*

RACHEL APT *is twenty-five. In vivid contrast to* HALINKA, *her hair is dark, her face plain and sharp. A sensitive, warm, responsible, hard-working girl, with a tide of hidden passion.*

RACHEL [*calling toward bedroom*]: David! [*She spies some things in a crate, sets down the suitcase to free a hand, reaches in and takes out a man's hat. Then she takes out a derby, next a boy's cap.* DAVID *enters from the right.*] Here. [*She hands* DAVID *the suitcase and the picture.*] Put these away in the closet. [*She takes the cap and slaps it on* DAVID'S *head.*] Your shelf . . . [*Following suit with the two hats*] Papa's shelf. Can you manage it all?

DAVID: Easy. [*He exits right.*]

[*There is a knock at the outside door.* RACHEL *crosses to open it, revealing* SYMKA BERSON*—a tense, pretty woman of thirty. She carries a potted plant, and is dressed for a gay occasion.*]

SYMKA: I'm Symka Berson—Dolek's wife, from upstairs.

RACHEL: Yes, hello, come in. You'll have to forgive us. The place is still in a mess.

SYMKA [*offering the plant*]: Something for luck in your new apartment.

RACHEL: How nice, how sweet of you. It's exactly what's missing.

SYMKA: I woke up this morning and decided I wanted to give someone a present. It's my anniversary.

RACHEL: *Mazel tov!*

SYMKA [*has been gazing around*]: You've got some lovely things. I was dying to come and look.

RACHEL [*conspiratorial*]: I know, I'm that way too. Nosy.

SYMKA: My mother had a chair like that. Dolek used to sit in it when he came to court me. Sit there and play the flute.

RACHEL: The flute?

SYMKA: He played the flute. He's very musical.

RACHEL: I hear him playing the piano. It always startles me. I see him on the stairs, he doesn't look like the kind of man who would play so . . . tenderly. I'm just jealous. I took lessons for years, it was hopeless. So—what can I give you? Coffee? Bite to eat?

SYMKA: I have to get back. Dolek isn't home yet. [*Nostalgically*] That chair. I had three different men asking for my hand. In marriage. One of them was a professor of zoology. The first minute I laid eyes on Dolek, I said good-by to all of them. Farewell, gentlemen. He played the flute, and it was like the pied piper. I just followed him.

RACHEL: Oh, I like that. I had a beau who played the saxophone. "The Blue Danube Waltz." I think it was the only song he knew. He came one night and played "The Blue Danube" three times, and then proposed to my sister.

SYMKA: He's usually home by this time, Dolek. Impossible man. Doesn't look crossing the streets. You don't suppose anything's wrong?

RACHEL: Don't worry.

SYMKA: Well, I do worry. Nothing I can do about it. I'm very high-strung. My watch stopped. That's a bad sign.

RACHEL [*dismissing it*]: Ehh. Come, a glass of tea.

SYMKA [*refusing*]: Dolek might come back and wonder where I am. [*She starts toward the door, but pauses at the chair, touching it fondly.*] Sometimes it seems yesterday I was parading around in pigtails, and psst, like that, here I am an old married woman. [*Smiles*] Maybe that's why my watch stopped. So I could catch my breath. [*Opening door*] Good luck.

RACHEL: Thank you. Come down and visit—any time. [SYMKA *is gone.* RACHEL *calls after her.*] And *mazel tov . . . mazel tov!*

[*She closes the door, then turns and takes up the mirror, a hammer, and a nail. As she prepares to hang the mirror, her sister,* HALINKA, *enters.*]

HALINKA: I've been putting things away all day, and my room still looks like a pigpen. What are you doing?

RACHEL: What does it look like I'm doing?

HALINKA: That's no place for a mirror.

RACHEL: This is the wall that needs it.

HALINKA: Don't be an idiot. It belongs over there.

RACHEL: I like it here.

HALINKA: That's ridiculous. A mirror ought to hang by the window. Here, give it to me.

RACHEL: Keep your hands off.

HALINKA: Over there. So that when you look at it, the light is on your face. Of course, that's the last thing in the world you'd want.

RACHEL: I'll kill you!

HALINKA [*reaching*]: Give me that. It's my mirror.

RACHEL: Get away!

HALINKA: It's mine, Father gave it to me!

[*Inner door flings open, and* MORDECAI *appears.*]

MORDECAI: Will you two stop that screaming? You know I'm trying to write!

HALINKA: "Trying" is good. My darling brother, the genius.

MORDECAI: Go to hell.

HALINKA [*lunges for mirror*]: Give me that!

[HALINKA *and* RACHEL *struggle over the mirror. The hall door opens, and* PAN APT *enters. The girls separate,* RACHEL *still clinging to the mirror.*]

[PAN APT *is a successful man: abstracted, elegantly dressed, excitable. An appraising way of looking at people, as though searching for the flaw in a dubious gem.*]

PAN APT: What's going on?

RACHEL [*kissing him*]: Hello, Father.

PAN APT: Somebody left potato peels all over the hall. I almost broke my neck. Disgraceful. [*Absently to* RACHEL] You need to comb your hair. It looks terrible. [*To all*] Have you heard? You heard what they're doing?

MORDECAI [*ironically*]: Which "they" is it this time, Father?

PAN APT [*letting* RACHEL *take his coat and hat*]: There's a rumor they're throwing all the Jews into a ghetto.

MORDECAI: *Wait* a minute, Father. All Jews? Uncle Albert in Cincinnati, too?

PAN APT: I heard it from Herr Gruber, the German trustee they put in charge of my store. He belongs in a jewelry business like I belong on a battleship.

RACHEL [*calling through doorway*]: David! Wash your hands, Father's home.

HALINKA: What's all this about a ghetto?

PAN APT [*embracing* HALINKA *protectively*]: It's all right, my baby. Nightingale, little bird, don't worry, it doesn't concern you Thank God I've put aside some money in my lifetime.

MORDECAI: Would you mind sticking to the subject for two minutes.

PAN APT: I told you, a ghetto, a ghetto. The Germans

are passing a law, all Jews have to live in a certain district. Here, this neighborhood. But it's all right, I'm making arrangements. He's got sharp ears, Herr Gruber. He heard the rustling of my money, and he said he could fix it for us to move to the Aryan section, or to Cracow, or even to Berlin if we wanted.

RACHEL: Dinner's almost ready. I made your favorite—sweet-and-sour stuffed cabbage.

PAN APT: I have to get back to the store. I just came for a minute to get something. That Meissen china figure, the shepherdess.

HALINKA: I don't think it's unpacked yet.

PAN APT: Do me a favor, princess, try to find it. I heard Herr Gruber mention he collects Meissen. I thought I might give it to him as a little present.

RACHEL: You have to eat something. How can you go without eating?

[HALINKA *searches the crates.*]

PAN APT: Mordecai, I wish you would give up this ridiculous idea of being a writer. It can only lead to poverty and trouble with women. And you, Halinka, my baby, wanting to be a singer. Drop that, my darling, and find yourself a nice husband. And you, poor Rachel . . . [*A painful pause.*]

RACHEL [*brightly*]: I'll set the table. It will only take a minute.

PAN APT [*to* MORDECAI]: They're shutting down the schools. I saw your old history teacher, he's working as a janitor.

HALINKA [*coming up with the shepherdess*]: Is this what you're looking for?

PAN APT: That's it. See if you can find a bit of paper. I hear everyone from fourteen to sixty is going to be registered for forced labor. [*To* MORDECAI] We have to make arrangements. You're a writer, not a . . . a carpenter.

MORDECAI: I thought you didn't want me to be a writer.

PAN APT: My dear boy, I want you to be whatever you want to be.

MORDECAI [*ironically*]: Thank you.

RACHEL: It's all ready.

PAN APT: I have to run.

RACHEL: Couldn't you just stay for—

[PAN APT *has already started to put on his coat.* RACHEL *helps him, and hands him his hat.*]

RACHEL: I'll save some to warm up for you when you get home.

[PAN APT *takes the figure from* HALINKA, *kisses her, and hurriedly exits.*]

DAVID [*appearing in doorway*]: Where's Papa? I'm starving. I thought dinner was ready.

RACHEL: In a few minutes.

[DAVID *vanishes.*]

HALINKA: I'm not eating in tonight. I've got a date.

MORDECAI: With whom?

HALINKA: Stefan, Rabbi Mazur's son, from upstairs.

MORDECAI [*grinning*]: Again? One week in the house, and it's starting already.

HALINKA: You should talk. What about you and his sister, Rutka?

MORDECAI: That's different. I'm looking for an intellectual relationship.

HALINKA: And what do you think I'm looking for?

MORDECAI [*mockingly*]: Pardon me. [*He exits.*]

HALINKA [*sees* RACHEL *putting up mirror at window*]: Rochele . . .

RACHEL: You're right about the mirror. It should go by the window.

HALINKA: I'm such a— I'm sorry.

RACHEL [*strokes* HALINKA'S *hair comfortingly*]: I know, I know.

[A *knock.* RACHEL *disengages herself and opens the hall door, revealing* DOLEK BERSON.]

BERSON: My wife thought I ought to let you know I got home all right. The Germans called a meeting.

RACHEL: A meeting? To announce about the ghetto?

BERSON: My dear Panna Apt, where do you get such ideas? Ghetto. Sounds like the Middle Ages. You ought to be ashamed of yourself. The Third

Reich is a modern nation. Everything up to the minute. Inventors of the glockenspiel and the diesel engine. Pioneers in preventive medicine. For years, doctors have thought typhus was carried by lice. Nonsense. Any good Nazi scientist can tell you—typhus is carried by Jews. You want to protect the public health? Simple. Put all the Jews in quarantine. *Not* a ghetto. The S.S. man made that quite clear. He distinctly said: "*Seuchensperrgebeit.*" Quarantine area.

RACHEL: When?

BERSON: Starting immediately. All the Jews in Warsaw—almost half a million—to be jammed into a hundred square blocks, like fish in a barrel.

[RACHEL *shakes her head in disbelief.*]

HALINKA: Would you like some coffee . . . beer?

BERSON: Thanks, beer.

[HALINKA *exits to get it.*]

[*To* RACHEL] They also ordered us to provide building materials—bricks, lime, mortar.

RACHEL: What for?

BERSON: Maybe they're planning to build us an opera house.

RACHEL: What happens now?

BERSON [*shrugs*]: I think I'll go to Australia.

[HALINKA *has entered, carrying a bottle of beer.*]

HALINKA: Why Australia?

BERSON: I've never seen a kangaroo.

[RACHEL *resumes setting the table, covertly watching* BERSON.]

HALINKA [*handing* BERSON *the beer*]: I always wanted to travel. [*She offers him the bottle opener.*]

BERSON: I've come to the conclusion it's my one real talent. [BERSON *waves away the opener, tries to open bottle with his teeth. In spite of his bravado, he fails, and ignominiously uses the opener.*] You learn all kinds of things, traveling.

[HALINKA *laughs.* BERSON *drinks.*]

RACHEL: We're having sweet-and-sour cabbage. Maybe you and your wife would like to have a bite with us?

BERSON: Thanks. I'm taking her out. It's our anniversary.

[RACHEL *nods and exits to the kitchen.* HALINKA *examines herself in the mirror.*]

HALINKA: I think I'll cut my hair.

BERSON: Don't. It's nice hair.

HALINKA: You think so? What I don't like are my eyes. I have cat's eyes. I think the eyes are the most important, I always judge people by their eyes. You have sensitive eyes.

[RACHEL *appears in the doorway.*]

RACHEL: The stove's gone out. I can't get it to light again.

BERSON: Here, let me take a look. [BERSON *exits.*]

[HALINKA *turns back to the mirror and begins to make up her face.* RACHEL *hesitates for a moment, watching.* HALINKA *is obviously pleased with the reflection of herself—the princess.* RACHEL *turns away, back into the kitchen. There is a knock at the hall door.*]

HALINKA [*calls*]: Yes . . . come in!

[STEFAN MAZUR *enters.*]

STEFAN: Ready?

HALINKA: In a second. [*She adds the finishing touches to her face, singing, quite aware of the effect on* STEFAN.]

STEFAN: You're lucky to be able to sing. I'd like to be an actor. But it takes training.

HALINKA [*turns, examining him*]: You've got the face for it. Especially the eyes. That's what's most important. You have sensitive eyes.

[*She has come close.* STEFAN *leans forward to kiss her, but she moves so that his lips barely brush her hair.* HALINKA *smiles, measuring him with her eyes.*]

STEFAN: What?

HALINKA: I never went out with a rabbi's son before.

STEFAN: A rabbi's son blows his nose just like everyone else.

HALINKA: Really? [*Calls*] Rachel? Stefan's here. I'm going.

[HALINKA *and* STEFAN *exit.* RACHEL *enters.*]

RACHEL: It's chilly out. Take your warm coat. [*She realizes* HALINKA *is gone.*]

[BERSON *enters.*]

BERSON: That's what happens, those little holes get clogged up. If it happens again, just take a hair-pin. [*He looks around.*] Where's your sister?

RACHEL: She left. Out on a date. It's fantastic. The Germans announce they're putting us in a ghetto, and everything goes right on.

BERSON: What do you expect?

RACHEL: I don't know. Something. Anything. Make a protest.

BERSON: There's an old saying, if you can't bite, don't show your teeth.

RACHEL: It's brilliant the way they do it, the Germans. Bit by bit, here and there. A dozen Jews grabbed in a restaurant and dragged away for forced labor. Ah, here it comes. But no. Quiet again. So, all right, it's not so bad. Bank accounts frozen. Quiet again. Public worship forbidden. Each time it hits a different group. Somebody yells, everybody else cries, *shaa!*—you'll only make trouble for the rest of us.

BERSON: Everybody worries about his own indigestion. It's human nature.

RACHEL: These little rules and regulations. Little stabs and jabs and pinpricks. Never mind, it's not serious, only a scratch. Nobody seems to realize, from enough pinpricks you can bleed to death. [*Pause. Then abruptly*] You're a lonely man?

BERSON: What do you mean?

RACHEL: I don't know, you look lonely.

BERSON: What a queer girl you are.

RACHEL: What do you think of my sister?

BERSON: Darling.

RACHEL: You're attracted to her.

BERSON: I'm almost twice her age.

RACHEL: What has that got to do with it?

BERSON: Also, I've got a wife.

RACHEL: Everybody falls in love with her. What is it?

BERSON [*dryly*]: I wouldn't know. Well . . . I have to be going.

RACHEL [*curt*]: Go. Nobody's keeping you.

BERSON: You're angry.

RACHEL: I'm not angry.

BERSON: What is it? I hurt your feelings?

RACHEL: Don't be a fool!

[*From somewhere off stage the sound of a scream is heard. A terrifying, sharp scream, again and again.*]

My God, what is it? [*Rushing to window*] Something terrible's going on outside.

BERSON: What?

RACHEL: I don't know. I can't see.

[*The shrieks continue. It is a woman's voice, high and unnerving.* RACHEL *grabs up a shawl and starts for the door.* BERSON *catches her wrist.*]

Let me go. Somebody needs help.

BERSON: Mind your own business.

[*The screaming continues.*]

RACHEL: Let . . . me . . . *go!*

BERSON: It's not healthy to be curious.

RACHEL [*struggling*]: Let go!

[*Suddenly the screaming cuts off, the echo hanging in mid-air.*]

[RACHEL *glares at* BERSON.] What are you, what's the matter with you? Aren't you human? Get out of here.

BERSON: What did you expect to do down there?

RACHEL: Get out.

[BERSON *hesitates, then exits, almost bumping into* RUTKA MAZUR, *a sturdy, direct girl in her twenties.*]

RUTKA: Did you hear that scream? What was it?

RACHEL: I couldn't see.

RUTKA: An animal? A person?

RACHEL: What do *you* think?

[MORDECAI *enters.*]

MORDECAI: They were beating up a woman on the street. I saw it from my window.

RUTKA: Nobody tried to stop them?

MORDECAI: What can you do?

RUTKA [*Trying to compose herself*]: I was looking for my brother, Stefan. He promised to come with me—we're having a meeting to set up soup kitchens for the refugees. You should come . . . [*Remembering* RACHEL] Both of you.

RACHEL: I was never in any organization. I don't know anything about it.

RUTKA: It's time you learned. [*To* MORDECAI] Come, please.

MORDECAI: Yes, all right. [*He takes up his coat.*]

RUTKA: Rachel?

RACHEL: I can't. I have to stay with David. [*To* MORDECAI] What about dinner?

MORDECAI: I'm not hungry.

RACHEL: I made cabbage.

MORDECAI: Later.

[*They exit.* DAVID *enters.*]

DAVID: Time to eat.

RACHEL: I'm putting it on the table.

DAVID: Where is everybody?

RACHEL [*sits, drawing him to her*]: David . . . do you know why we had to move?

DAVID: They took our place for the *Wienerschnitzel* to live in.

RACHEL: Tell me, has anybody said anything to you at school about . . . what's happening?

DAVID: What do you mean? About the Nazis? They

don't like us. They're going to make a wall around us.

RACHEL: A *wall?*

DAVID: A wall, a fence to keep us in. [*Matter of fact*] Did you make dessert?

[RACHEL *looks at him and finds herself suddenly struggling not to weep.*]

RACHEL [*furiously*]: How many times have I asked you to tuck in your sweater? Go and wash your face. It's filthy!

DAVID: What's the matter?

RACHEL: I said go and wash!

DAVID: All right. What's the matter with you, anyhow? [DAVID *exits.*]

[RACHEL *rises and begins to clear away the extra place settings.*]

RACHEL: David . . . [*she leaves the dishes and silver in a heap, and strays to the mirror. She begins to fix her hair, unconsciously using the gestures of* HALINKA, *letting herself drift in a fantasy of dazzling beauty. Then the dream snaps, and she turns.*] David!

[DAVID *enters, gazing at* RACHEL *inquiringly. She sweeps him into her arms, hugging him desperately, as though to save him from drowning. Then she releases him with a whack on the behind.*] Go sit down.

DAVID: What's for dessert?

RACHEL: The Germans are shivering in Russia? Couldn't we make it worse for them? Maybe mutilate the furs some way so they can't use them. There must be a way.
BERSON: Simple. Here, I'll show you.

ACT I: *Scene 5*

REB MAZUR: Blessed art thou, O Lord our God, King of the universe, Who has created joy and gladness, bride-groom and bride, mirth and exultation, pleasure and delight, love and brotherhood, peace and fellowship.

ACT I: *Scene 6*

RACHEL [*exiting into kitchen*]: None of your business.

[DAVID *hides.* RACHEL *enters carrying a pot—looks for* DAVID, *sighs, and crosses to the table.*]

DAVID [*slips up behind her—a deep, startling basso*]: *What's for dessert?*

RACHEL [*jumps*]: Oi! [*She turns on* DAVID.] I'll give you—

[*She grabs at him. He evades her, leading her a wild laughing chase.*] I'll give you dessert!

[*She captures him at last. Laughing, they sink down on the couch.*] Cookies. I made almond cookies. Idiot. [*Smoothing his hair*] Go sit down.

[*Lights dim out on the scene.*]

[SCENE 3]

The street, six months later. A chill early morning in autumn.

Looming over the scene is the Wall. It is built of brick, a good three feet higher than a man's head, with jagged fragments of glass along the top. It spans upstage from the rear of the apartment house to the rear of the bakery, blocking off the alley.

The final work on the Wall is still going on. At right is a pile of bricks—and somewhere off behind the house is a labor battalion. We can hear the clatter of shovels and the scrape of masons' trowels.

*Two German soldiers—*SERGEANT *and* PRIVATE *—are just finishing putting up a loud-speaker in* *the linden tree. As the soldiers gather up their ladder, tools, roll of wire, and exit,* DOLEK BERSON *enters, trundling a wheelbarrow. He wears the classic badge of the ghetto Jew—an arm band with a Star of David. Setting his barrow down near the pile of bricks,* BERSON *crosses to peer at the loud-speaker, perched among the linden branches like a malignant bird.*

VOICE [*from off right*]: *Schneller!* Bricks!

[MENKES *comes out of the bakery and crosses to join* BERSON.]

BERSON: Did you ever see such a tree? A miracle. In the middle of November, it begins to bear fruit.

MENKES: What is it for?

BERSON: Playing us Strauss waltzes.

[FISHEL SHPUNT *enters. He too wears a Star arm band, and has a pile of others draped over his arm.*]

SHPUNT [*looking at loud-speaker*]: Ah-hah, they're starting already.

MENKES: Starting what?

SHPUNT: Whatever they're starting. [*Waving an arm band*] Merchandise, Menkes. I've got merchandise. You've been putting me off for a week. This is the day. Any Jew found without an arm band will be arrested. [*Displaying his styles*] Hand-embroidered for five zlotys, plain for two.

[MENKES *pays* SHPUNT, *and takes the arm band —starts to put it on, then lets his hand drop helplessly.*]

MENKES: I can't.

SHPUNT: Here, I'll put it on for you. Free service.

[SHPUNT *slides the badge on* MENKES'S *arm.* MENKES *looks at it bitterly.*]

SHPUNT: You'll get used to it.

MENKES: Never! [*He struggles to control himself. To* BERSON] What do you feel? Shame? Pride? You carry a mark, like they spit on you. Are you the same man?

BERSON: Yes.

MENKES: No!

VOICE: [*from off right*]: Bricks! Ho, let's have those bricks!

BERSON: Coming!

VOICE: Bricks!

BERSON [*sweetly, murderously*]: Coming, coming . . . [*He wheels off his barrow.*]

SHPUNT: Listen, Menkes, it's getting late. The sun is up, it's time for morning prayers.

MENKES: Yes, all right. [*He darts a nervous look around, then exits into bakery with* SHPUNT.]

[*From the left, the* KOGAN *family enters. They are dressed neatly, stiffly, a cameo of small-town respectability.* PAN KOGAN *carries a suitcase and an umbrella;* PANI KOGAN *primly carries an incongruous sack. Eight-year-old* REGINA *carries a doll. They approach the closed door of* MENKES'S *bakery, and* PAN KOGAN *knocks. Finally* MENKES *opens the door a crack.*]

What do you want? It's too early, I'm not open yet.

PAN KOGAN: If you'll be so kind, you don't happen to have an apartment for rent?

MENKES: No.

PAN KOGAN [*quickly*]: Please. Maybe you heard a customer mention something. I know how it is. I also had a store—Kogan's Apothecary, in Otwosk. You haven't got a room?

MENKES [*not unkindly*]: I'm a bachelor, I live in a hole in the wall.

PAN KOGAN [*has taken out his wallet, and produces a snapshot*]: See? Am I lying? That was my shop, that's my name on the sign, Kogan. The Germans came and threw us out. Didn't even give me time to close the windows.

MENKES: Why don't you try around the corner, at the schoolhouse? I hear they made it into a shelter for refugees.

PAN KOGAN: We went there last night. Everybody pushing, shoving, on top of one another, like animals. Not a place for respectable people.

MENKES: I don't know of anything. Wait a minute . . .

[*From left,* MORDECAI *enters, wheeling a barrow.* MENKES *has reached inside, and now brings forth a bun, which he hands to* REGINA.]

Here, you're a good girl, here's a bun for you.

[REGINA *looks to her father for permission.*]

PAN KOGAN: It's not necessary.

[MENKES *forces the bun into* REGINA'S *hand.*]

What do you say?

REGINA: Thank you.

[MENKES *starts to close the door.*]

PAN KOGAN: A space in the attic? An empty woodshed?

MENKES: I don't have anything. What do you want me to do?

PAN KOGAN: You don't need, perhaps, an assistant?

MENKES: You're not a baker.

PAN KOGAN: You'll teach me, I'll be a baker.

[MENKES *starts to close the door.*]

PAN KOGAN [*violently*]: Don't make me beg!

[*The door is shut.*]

I'm a respectable man!

PANI KOGAN: Don't worry. We'll find something.

[*She takes* REGINA'S *hand, and the* KOGANS *exit, right.*]

[PAN APT *emerges from the house, crosses down,*

and stands watching MORDECAI *load his barrow.*]

MORDECAI: Hello, Father.

PAN APT: Enjoying yourself? [*Pause.*] For the last time, let me buy you an exemption. I'll arrange it, and you'll come and work with me in the store.

MORDECAI: No, thanks.

PAN APT: It hurts me to see you. A boy with your talent.

MORDECAI: What talent?

PAN APT: Your writing.

MORDECAI: What writing? I never wrote a line. It was a fake, a joke! I used to close the door and sit up there reading cheap novels.

PAN APT: You're saying it out of spite, to spite me—

MORDECAI: This is the first honest work I ever did in my life.

PAN APT:—because you've got a stubborn streak! God in heaven, what pleasure does it give you to eat my heart out? [*Cajoling*] Mordecai . . . let me get you the papers. What's wrong with it? It's the times we live in. People used to pray to God, now they pray to papers. [*He takes a pass out of his pocket and flourishes it.*] Look. Go to the gate and show my little paper. I can go out, go to the store, manage my business. [*Gently*] Let me get you the papers.

MORDECAI: Do me a favor. Forget it.

PAN APT [*a bitter cry*]: Go ahead, cut off your nose to spite your face! [*He catches* MORDECAI'S *jacket.*] What did I ever do to you? What? *I'm not dirt, I'm your father!* [*He slaps* MORDECAI'S *face.*]

MORDECAI: Since I was ten, nothing I did ever satisfied you. Goddammit, for once in my life, let me do something on my own!

PAN APT [*slowly releasing him*]: I have to go. It's time to open the store. Mordecai . . . ? [*Pause.*] Look at your hands, don't you have a pair of gloves? I'll bring you a pair of gloves. [PAN APT *exits.*]

[*During the following, a man enters, raps softly on the bakery door, and is admitted. A few moments later,* STEFAN *comes out of the house, crosses to the bakery, knocks, then signals* REB MAZUR, *who crosses from the house and enters the bakery with his son.*]

[BERSON *enters from right, wiping his brow with his shirt tail.*]

BERSON: They're laying the last row. A few more loads and we'll be finished.

MORDECAI: The other crew, over by the Saxon Gardens, finished yesterday.

VOICE [*off*]: Bricks! Let's have those bricks!

[MORDECAI *takes up barrow and starts off right.*]

BERSON [*following*]: So now the rest of the city can relax. They're safe from contamination.

[BERSON *is intercepted by* KATZ, *who has entered from right.*]

KATZ: Berson . . . I want to talk to you.

BERSON [*sitting wearily*]: So talk.

KATZ: About our situation as Jews . . . Am I boring you?

BERSON: You haven't started talking yet. Don't be offended until you hear snoring.

KATZ: You're a clever man with your hands, Berson. We could use you.

BERSON: I'm not a joiner, Katz, you know that.

KATZ: What the hell do you think you can do alone?

BERSON: Survive.

KATZ: You want a life preserver? [*He whips out a pocket knife, flicking open the blade.*] This is your life preserver. [BERSON *looks at the knife with a dry smile and rises.*]

[KATZ grabs BERSON's *arm.*] Afraid?

[BERSON *patiently releases* KATZ's *hand.*]

[*From left, a German* PRIVATE *and a* SERGEANT *enter, crossing to the bakery.*]

[*Seeing the Germans,* BERSON *swiftly reaches out, closing the knife.*]

[*German* PRIVATE *indicates the bakery door.* SERGEANT *bangs on it.*]

SERGEANT: Open up!

[*Pause. He bangs again.*]

Open up!

[*The bakery door opens slowly. The* SERGEANT *slams it back all the way, and kicks open the other door.*]

Out. Everybody out.

[*Ten men file out of the bakery, their heads covered with prayer shawls, their brows adorned with the small black boxes of their phylacteries. Among them are* STEFAN, REB MAZUR, SHPUNT, *and* MENKES.]

[BERSON *enters and joins* MORDECAI, *watching.*]

SERGEANT: Saying your prayers? Don't let us interrupt you. Go ahead. [*As no one moves*] Go ahead. Pray.

[REB MAZUR *starts to chant the morning prayers, and one by one the others join in.*]

[*The Germans watch. News of what is happening has filtered into the apartment house, and the occupants begin to come out, keeping their distance, tense and apprehensive. First* RACHEL *and* HALINKA, *then* DAVID *and* RUTKA.]

SERGEANT [*cutting off the chanting*]: All right, enough. Enough.

[*The praying trails into silence.*]

Who is the rabbi here?

[*A pause. No one looks at* REB MAZUR. *The* SERGEANT *waits.*]

SHPUNT [*finally*]: I. I am the rabbi.

SERGEANT [*drawing his pistol*]: Out here, please. Step back, give him room.

[SHPUNT *shuffles forward and stands alone, a preposterous caricature. The* SERGEANT *draws a careful bead.*] Dance!

[SHPUNT *raises his misshapen face, his eyebrows lifting questioningly.*]

You're not deaf? I said dance, Rabbi!

[*Slowly, with a reminiscent expression, as if to say: "Oh yes, this is something from my boyhood,"* SHPUNT *begins a clumsy jigging and hopping, a wierd, froglike gavotte.*]

SERGEANT [*smiling*]: Faster!

[SHPUNT *increases his tempo.*]

Come, Rabbi, a little joy, a little gaiety!

[SHPUNT *jigs and whirls. The Germans are delighted. The* SERGEANT *laughs, fighting to catch his breath.*] All right . . . all right, Rabbi. You can stop. [*He turns to the others.*] Go home. You know public worship is forbidden. [*He sighs, wipes his eyes, and, still chuckling, exits with* PRIVATE.]

[*There is a curious, embarrassed silence.* MENKES *goes back into his shop.* RACHEL *follows him.*

The others melt away. KATZ *stands confronting* BERSON*—a long exchange of hard glances between them, neither giving ground. Then* BERSON *crosses to the brick pile, and* KATZ *exits.*]

[MORDECAI *catches up with* RUTKA.]

MORDECAI: Rutka. Will I see you tonight?

RUTKA: I can't.

MORDECAI: Rutka . . .

RUTKA: Don't.

MORDECAI [*reaching for her hand*]: Please . . . I must see you!

RUTKA [*jerking away*]: Leave me alone. After seeing that, how can you think about dates? [*she hurries off.*]

[MORDECAI *returns to his barrow.*]

[RACHEL *emerges from the bakery.*]

RACHEL [*pausing before* BERSON]: When Shpunt danced, you were smiling. Why?

[BERSON *shrugs.*]

You have no heart at all, have you?

BERSON: Because I laugh? That's the way I am. If I try to be like someone else, who will be like me?

[PAN APT *darts in, hurrying up to* BERSON *and* RACHEL.]

PAN APT: Something's happening. Mordecai . . . [*Bewilderedly*]: I don't understand. I went up to the entrance at Panska. All of a sudden they've got barbed wire across the street, German guards, machine guns. I went up to the guard and gave him my pass. Absolutely official. [*He shows pass.*] "The bearer has permission—" Official signature, everything. I give it to the guard, he hands it back to me. Worthless. How can it be worthless? It has an official signature, it cost me a fortune.

RACHEL: What about the other entrances? Krochmalna Street—

PAN APT: Closed! Everything's closed. [*To* MORDECAI] What's happening?

VOICE [*off*]: Ho! Bricks!

PAN APT: How can I go to business? We're locked in.

VOICE: Ho! Let's have those bricks!

PAN APT: *What's happening?*

MORDECAI: I'm sorry, Father. I have to go back to work.

LOUD-SPEAKER [*abruptly, a mechanical rasp, shockingly powerful*]: Attention! Attention! By order of the occupation authorities, the Jewish District is hereby closed. Any Jew attempting to go beyond the Wall will be shot.

[*Everyone stares fascinatedly at the linden tree.*]

VOICE: Ho! Bricks!

LOUD-SPEAKER: Attention! The Jewish District is closed. Any Jew attempting to go outside the Wall will be shot.

VOICE: *Ho—bring those bricks!*

BERSON [*savagely—a cry that seems to rip up from his soul*]: Y-e-ssss! [*He wrenches to his feet, and starts off right.*] Coming . . .

[*The* LOUD-SPEAKER *blares a tinny German waltz.*]

[*The lights dim out.*]

[SCENE 4]

The street. The following spring.

It is almost twilight. Beyond the Wall, Warsaw stretches away in the gathering shadows, distant as another planet.

From left, the KOGAN *family enter.*

PAN KOGAN: Warsaw. What am I doing in Warsaw?

PANI KOGAN: A city of beggars. Everywhere you turn, somebody's got his hand out.

[REGINA *has strayed off. She stoops, absorbed, letting her doll fall forgotten.*]

PAN KOGAN: Regina!

PANI KOGAN: What are you doing, darling? Come away, you'll get dirty.

REGINA [*without obeying*]: Yes, Mama.

PAN KOGAN: Is my tie straight? [*He lets* PANI KOGAN *fuss with it.*] People respect appearances. [*He breaks off abruptly, as a* WOMAN IN A BABUSHKA *enters.* KOGAN *approaches her, whipping open his coat, displaying clothing pinned inside.*] Bargains, my dear lady. Shirt for your husband, pajamas . . . [*The* WOMAN *looks at his wares casually, hardly pausing.*]

[*He offers the tie he is wearing.*] A nice necktie? Real silk.

WOMAN IN A BABUSHKA: I need a husband, not a necktie.

[*The* WOMAN *starts to move on.* KOGAN *steers her toward his wife.*]

PAN KOGAN: Maybe something for yourself. A nice dress. Show her, show her!

[*With embarrassment, as though forced to reveal her naked body,* PANI KOGAN *opens her coat, showing the clothes pinned inside.*]

Blouse? Stockings?

WOMAN IN A BABUSHKA: How much is the doll?

PAN KOGAN: The doll? Two zlotys. [*Pause.*] One zloty.

PANI KOGAN: You don't want it. The head is cracked.

PAN KOGAN: It's nothing, it can be fixed.

PANI KOGAN: Here, a lovely blouse, hand-embroidered. [*Hugging the doll*] It's broken . . . it's not for sale.

PAN KOGAN: It's for sale. [*To his wife*] She doesn't need the doll. She doesn't play with it any more. [*To* REGINA] Do you need the doll?

[REGINA *stares at him expressionlessly, then shakes her head "no."*]

See? She's a big girl, she's too old for dolls.

[*His desperate eyes are pleading for some sign. But his wife's face is set. She gazes through him, clutching the doll as though it were a baby.*]

You'll drive me out of my mind. [*Turns to* WOMAN] It's not for sale.

[*The* WOMAN *sniffs and starts off,* PAN KOGAN *chasing after her.*]

How about a nice umbrella? [*Struggling to open it*] Perfect condition . . . not a single hole in it. Look, everything perfect . . .

[WOMAN *exits.* PAN KOGAN *returns, slowly closing the umbrella.*]

PANI KOGAN [*gently*]: I'm sorry.

PAN KOGAN [*pats her arm*]: Come, we'll try Mila Street, there's more traffic.

[*They start off,* REGINA *trailing.* BERSON *enters.*]

Bargains . . . good clothing, cheap . . .

[BERSON *shakes his head, and continues past.*]

[PAN *and* PANI KOGAN *exit.* REGINA *turns, runs after* BERSON, *and tugs at his sleeve.*]

BERSON [*turning*]: Yes?

[REGINA *gazes steadily and silently at him.*]

Yes, what is it? What do you want?

[*Pause. Then* REGINA *slowly puts out her hand.* BERSON *looks at her, fishes in his pocket, and gives her a coin.*]

PANI KOGAN'S VOICE [*calling from off*]: Regina!

[REGINA *runs out.*]

[BERSON *crosses to the bakery and knocks at the door.*]

BERSON: Menkes? [*As* MENKES *opens the door*] Do you know where I can find Fishel Shpunt?

MENKES: I haven't seen him.

BERSON: If he comes around, tell him I'm looking for him, it's important.

[MENKES *nods and shuts the door.* BERSON *starts down to the street, as* REB MAZUR *enters.*]

Reb Mazur, have you seen Shpunt?

REB MAZUR: Shpunt? No. Dolek, listen, from a reliable source I just heard the Pope himself is arranging a meeting in Switzerland to make peace.

BERSON: Good. Tell him he's got my blessing.

REB MAZUR: Maybe he's gone, Shpunt. Maybe the Germans took him for forced labor. Wait, God will punish them.

BERSON: God? Is there a God? What is He? A practical joker?

REB MAZUR: What's the matter, Dolek? What's wrong? [*As* BERSON *turns away*] I heard this morning, from Sweden they're sending an envoy to try and save the Jews.

BERSON: You heard! And I heard from America they're sending us two thousand hammers—to knock the dreams out of our heads! [*More gently*] Rabbi, you're a fine man, but you're like a telephone. You repeat whatever is whispered into you. Have you got a match? [*Painfully*] Rabbi . . . my wife is sick.

REB MAZUR: Symka?

BERSON: She's got typhus.

REB MAZUR: God forbid . . .

BERSON: Lying up there burning. Touch her cheek, it's like a forest fire. The doctor's supposed to report it, and then they . . . send her to a hospital. [*A harsh little laugh.*] Have you seen our hospital? It's a marvel. Patients lying two in a bed, crammed in the corridors. No medicine, no X ray, not even a forceps. When they had to move behind the Wall, the Nazis lightened their load by confiscating the equipment. Dear Jews, sweet Jews, let us shorten your agony. And they gave us that stripped and stinking hospital. A monument to compassion! [*He draws a trembling breath. When he can trust himself to speak again, the mockery is gone.*] She's in a panic, Symka. Scared to death I'll let them send her. Lies up there biting the sheets to keep from screaming. Terrible. Because, let me tell you, Rabbi, she's not a weak woman. Tense, tight as a spring, I mean, sometimes it can get on your nerves. But I . . . remember when she went to have all those tests, and she found out she'd never be able to have a baby, and . . . came home to tell me. Very quiet, no tears, not a tear, nothing. All she said was: "I'm so sorry." She said: "Well, now you'll have to be my husband *and* my children." There was never a day she didn't try to find some way to get it through my head, there was love in the house. And that takes strength, believe me. [*With painful effort*] Because I'm . . . restless, you know? A restless man. When I met her I didn't have a groszy in my pocket. All I had was my youth, and I kept that for myself. What have I ever given her? *What the hell have I ever given her?* A bunch of violets for her birthday! [*Pause. Then evenly*] But this is one thing she can depend on. She's not going to that hospital. They try to send her, it will be over my dead body.

REB MAZUR: How are you going to keep them from—

BERSON: I got the doctor to agree not to report it.

REB MAZUR: Thank the Lord for a little human kindness.

BERSON: Human kindness is like everything else these days. You get it at smuggler's prices.

REB MAZUR: You said the doctor—

BERSON: For two hundred zlotys. Don't look so shocked, Rabbi. The shark eats the herring, and the herring eats where he can. [*He looks off—calls*] Shpunt! Shpunt!

[FISHEL SHPUNT *enters from left.*]

I've been looking all over for you. Listen, I need money, I want to sell my piano.

SHPUNT [*with a queer glint in his eye*]: You didn't hear? I'm out of the furniture business.

BERSON: What are you talking about?

SHPUNT [*sings*]:

> Should I be a rabbi,
> I don't know any Torah;
> Should I be a merchant,
> I don't have any goods.

[*Gaily*] The Germans came and took the furniture. Everything. Ptttt! [*Sings*]

> And oats I don't have,
> And groats I don't have,
> And I'd like a drink of whisky!

BERSON [*impatiently*]: Look, Fishel, stop the comedy—

SHPUNT: So now I'm in a new profession. The greeting line. I greet my friends. Hello, good morning—

BERSON: All right, enough.

SHPUNT: Long live Fishel Shpunt, son of Mendel the ragpicker, king of the greeting business!

[*Sings*]

Fire, fire, brothers,
Our little town is burning down!

BERSON: I'm in a hurry, Shpunt, I've got no time to—

SHPUNT: Business comes first, gentlemen . . . business . . .

[SHPUNT *crosses toward German* PRIVATE *who has entered. With friendly alacrity,* SHPUNT *suddenly tips his hat and offers his hand. Without thinking, the German* PRIVATE *take it.*]

[*A litany*] Hello, *Guten Tag,* good afternoon, how do you do, *sholem aleichem*—

PRIVATE [*realizing he's been tricked, jerks away his hand and roughly grabs* SHPUNT *by his coat*]: What the hell is the idea?

[*The* PRIVATE *starts to reach for his pistol.*]

[*His coat still twisted in the German's iron grasp,* SHPUNT *begins his froglike dance. There is a poised moment, as the* GERMAN *weighs vengeance.*]

SHPUNT [*sings*]:

Yum di peetle-dum
Yeedle deedle die!

PRIVATE [*in spite of himself, grins faintly at the spectacle, and shoves* SHPUNT *away*]: Imbecile!
[SHPUNT *stumbles, still cavorting in his weird, comic jig. Laughing now, the German* PRIVATE *jams* SHPUNT's *hat down over his eyes and exits.*]

BERSON: An interesting business.

SHPUNT: The only thing is, it doesn't pay. To make a living, I have to have a sideline.

BERSON: What sort of sideline?

SHPUNT [*sings*]:

Should I be a tailor,
I don't have any thread;
Should I be a baker,
I don't have any bread.

[*Mysteriously*] What for a sideline? What? [*He produces a wig from his pocket.*] Wigs. Wigs. Summer is coming. The typhus will be getting worse. Hundreds of ladies will be losing their hair. And what is more hideous than a bald woman? So I will satisfy the vanity of the ladies!

REB MAZUR [*low*]: Stop . . . stop it! [*He darts a glance at* BERSON, *whose face is impassive.*]

SHPUNT: The pious are cutting off their beards. There's plenty of hair available. Absolutely first-class. All the latest styles. [*He takes off his hat and puts on the wig.*] Guaranteed lice free. Easy to clean—a little benzine. Won't slip or slide. You can comb it, brush it, curl it, pull it.

REB MAZUR: Disgusting.

SHPUNT: Hoo-ha! Because your nose is delicate, the world should stop sweating? And building a wall around your own kind—that's less disgusting? [*Mimics astigmatic bewilderment*] Wall, wall? What wall? Sha, pay no attention.

[*Croons*]

Sleep, little bird, sleep!
Shut your little eyes, shut!

[*Going off*]

Ayleh lulu lu . . .
Ayleh lulu lu . . .

[*Lights dim out on the street—and come up on the balcony as* MORDECAI *emerges.* RUTKA *follows him.*]

MORDECAI: Leave me alone! Just go away and leave me alone.

RUTKA: Mordecai, my darling, don't.

MORDECAI: I've asked you to marry me. I don't want to be kissed and sent to bed like a child. I want an answer.

RUTKA: Please.

MORDECAI: You promised me an answer!

RUTKA [*with violence*]: Why do you go on pretending the Wall doesn't exist? God damn them and God damn their Wall!

MORDECAI [*an urgent whisper*]: I love you. I love you . . .

RUTKA: How long can love last, in this cage? Give me a little time, don't ask me today.

MORDECAI: How long am I supposed to wait?

RUTKA: Please, not today.

MORDECAI: I'm tired of waiting!

[*She catches* MORDECAI'*s arms, and they embrace, just as* RACHEL *enters from left.* RACHEL *sees the embrace, hesitates a beat, then starts up toward the house.*]

[*Off left, a sound of children's shouts and laughter is heard.*]

[*On the balcony,* MORDECAI *has torn away, and plunged inside.*]

RUTKA: Mordecai! Mordecai!

[*She follows him—lights dimming out on the balcony.*]

RACHEL [*calling*]: David! David!

[DAVID *enters from upstage, behind the bakery.*] Where have you been? You look as though you've been crawling through the sewers.

DAVID: I tore my pants.

RACHEL: Let me see. [*Inspecting*] You're impossible. Aie, what am I going to do with you? [*She shakes him, grinning.*] Aie, what am I going to do with him? [*She gives him a fond whack.*] Inside, I want you to get to bed at a decent hour. School starts tomorrow.

DAVID [*groans*]: School.

RACHEL: And, David, remember: it's something you don't talk about. You understand that? A secret.

DAVID: Why should I keep it a secret? If the Germans find out, they'll close the school, we won't have to study.

RACHEL [*laughs and whacks him again*]: Inside.

[DAVID *turns toward the door, just as* BERSON *emerges.*]

DAVID [*his hands going to imaginary gun holsters as he draws*]: I been lookin' for you . . .

[BERSON *stops, then slowly turns.*]

Reach for your gun.

[*They both draw imaginary six-shooters and fire madly as they advance on each other. They stop.* DAVID *turns away, then suddenly wheels back and fires a last shot.* BERSON *collapses to the ground dramatically.*]

DAVID [*to* RACHEL]: He can wiggle his ears. [*To* BERSON.] Show her.

[BERSON *sits up and obliges.*]

RACHEL: Brilliant.

BERSON [*to* DAVID]: I've got a present for you. [*He makes a magician's pass, and produces an egg.*]

DAVID: An egg!

RACHEL: An egg!

[DAVID *has snatched it, and dashed into the house.* RACHEL *moves to follow him.*]

BERSON: How's the new schoolteacher?

RACHEL: I've got nineteen children coming. Feel my hands, they're like ice. You'd think I was going to my first dance.

BERSON: Thank you for going in to sit with Symka this morning.

RACHEL: The doctor came again? What did he say?

BERSON: Apparently it's a long, ugly business. She needs a special diet—sugar, glucose injections. Maybe I'll have some money from my piano. When that's gone . . .

RACHEL: How is she?

BERSON: She is possessed by the idea she's going to die. Did she speak about it this morning?

RACHEL: All she spoke about was you. She said: "I'm married to him five and a half years, and he's a stranger, I don't know him."

BERSON: What makes you think to marry is to know? Marriage is two people walking down a blind alley, holding hands to pretend they are not alone.

RACHEL [*angrily*]: She adores you. Sit with her, for God's sake! Talk to her. Give yourself!

BERSON: I always seem to upset you.

RACHEL: So damned self-contained.

BERSON: Is that the reason?

RACHEL: No, that's not the reason. I don't know the reason. Forgive me, I've had a long day. [RACHEL *exits into the house.*]

[BERSON *starts across the street, right—where* PAN APT *enters.*]

PAN APT: Ah, Berson! Good.

BERSON: You want to see me?

PAN APT: Not near the house. [*Drawing him away*] My dear Berson. [*He offers* BERSON *a cigarette, not noticing that he is already smoking.*] I have not even told my children what I am about to tell you. I don't understand my children these days. No respect, no obedience. Even the little one doesn't listen to me. And I worship them. I would break my arms for them. [*Pacing restlessly*] Last week a German slapped my face because I forgot to tip my hat. And this morning another German slapped me because I tipped my hat. You've had this experience?

BERSON: The day the Germans marched into Warsaw, I stopped wearing a hat.

PAN APT: And in the winter?

BERSON: My ears freeze.

PAN APT: I am fifty-two years old. An authority on precious gems and Persian miniatures. Also something of an amateur expert on insect life. Bees, butterflies, ants, and so forth. You can learn from the ants, Berson. Amazing discipline. [*Pause.*] I've decided to leave the Ghetto.

BERSON: Where will you go?

PAN APT: I have Polish friends. For the last three months I've been studying Catholic ritual. Oh, I'll manage. There are just a few things. I'll be needing certain . . . medical attention. I have to find a reliable doctor, preferably a plastic surgeon.

BERSON: Why are you telling this to—

PAN APT: Also, I need a Polish identity card. An authentic one, not a forgery. The card of someone who has died, or left the country. I understand they're for sale, if you know the right people.

BERSON: Why come to me?

PAN APT: You have curiosity. A man with curiosity discovers where to get hold of things.

[BERSON *rises and starts back toward the house. The door opens and* SYMKA *appears.*]

Berson?

BERSON: I'll think about it.

[PAN APT *exits right.*]

SYMKA: Dolek . . .

BERSON: What are you doing out of bed?

SYMKA: I was going to look for you. I think my fever has gone down. Comes and goes. I'd give anything for a piece of candy. You know I've always had this terrible sweet tooth. [*A sudden sob.*] Dolek, what's going to happen to me?

BERSON: Shhh, it's all right, don't worry about it.

SYMKA: You won't let them send me—

BERSON [*holding her comfortingly*]: No. I promised. Didn't I promise? [*Suddenly he sweeps her up in his arms.*] Come, back to bed.

SYMKA [*laughing*]: Put me down.

[BERSON *gently sets her down, and they exit into the house.*]

[RUTKA *appears upstage.* KATZ *enters from left. A man crosses past the bakery.* KATZ *starts to talk, but* RUTKA *stops him with a warning signal.*]

RUTKA: We're giving a concert tomorrow night. The Mendelssohn Concerto. I thought you might like to— [*She breaks off, as the man exits.*]

[REB MAZUR *emerges from the house.*]

KATZ [*darts a look around, then takes out a paper*]: Here. Editorial for the newspaper. News from our friends in Bialystok.

[RUTKA *swiftly tucks it in her dress.*]

REB MAZUR: What news?

KATZ: A massacre of the Jews in Bialystok!

RUTKA: A what?

REB MAZUR: Nothing. Believe me, it was nothing. The Community Council has positive proof. A few drunken soldiers got out of hand.

KATZ: I heard it was a massacre.

REB MAZUR: And I have heard that those rumors were started by a certain faction among us, to stir up the people, get them alarmed.

KATZ: Are you accusing—

REB MAZUR: Listen, Katz, I know you since you were in diapers. And even then you were a trouble-maker.

[CLERK *enters from upstage, and joins the circle.*]

KATZ: Bialystok was a warning. We have to get together and give them a smack while we've still got the strength.

REB MAZUR: Not so fast, my friend. We'll start something, and innocent people will pay for it.

CLERK: By the Brushmakers Factory a few nights ago somebody poured boiling water on a German patrol. They took twenty women and children—machine guns—ba-ba-ba-ba-ba! Finished.

KATZ: For God's sake, wake up!

[*Upstage, from behind the bakery, a German* SERGEANT *appears. He stands listening, unseen by the others.*]

REB MAZUR: All right, Katz. So we should resist, eh? Simple, eh? The German command in Warsaw has an army of S.S. men, with machine guns, flame throwers, tanks, armored cars. The Gestapo. The Polish police. Yes. All right. So you tell me how to resist. With what? Our teeth? Slogans? Umbrellas? Tell me! I will do whatever you tell me!

KATZ: We'll fight them with our bare hands!

[KATZ's *eye catches the* SERGEANT, *who casually comes down to the street.*]

SERGEANT [*to* KATZ, *pleasantly*]: You know there is a regulation forbidding political discussion.

[*Without warning, he brings his knee up into* KATZ's *groin.* KATZ *doubles over.* SERGEANT *turns to the others. Quietly*] I give you exactly five seconds to clear the street.

[*The others melt away.* REB MAZUR *starts up toward the house. The* SERGEANT *goes off.* KATZ *struggles agonizedly to climb the steps.*]

[*At the door,* REB MAZUR *turns, making a half-gesture, as though to help* KATZ.]

KATZ [*a fierce whisper*]: With our bare hands . . .

[*He doubles over with pain.*]

[*The lights fade out.*]

[SCENE 5]

The APT *apartment. An evening, the following winter.*

STEFAN *is watching* HALINKA *at the mirror. She is wearing a party frock, an attempt at sophistication which simply makes her look very young.* STEFAN'S *ordinary suit has been converted into an improvised uniform by a military belt, a club, and a yellow brassard.* HALINKA *is trying on his blue police cap.*

STEFAN: It's late. I have to go on duty.

HALINKA [*taking off the cap*]: Officer Mazur, Jewish police. [*She hands the cap back to* STEFAN.]

STEFAN: I haven't seen my father yet. I don't think he'll approve.

HALINKA: Why?

STEFAN: Well, you know, a rabbi . . . He doesn't like the club. He says Cain carries a club.

HALINKA: Cain?

STEFAN: You know, Cain and Abel? In the Bible. You've got blonde hairs on your upper lip. Like the fuzz on a peach.

[HALINKA *measures him, smiling faintly.*]

What?

HALINKA: That uniform. You look like you ought to be chasing Charlie Chaplin.

STEFAN: The Germans told us we'd be able to, you know, make life a little easier. Protect our families. [*He moves close, his hand tentatively reaching out to touch* HALINKA'*s shoulder.*]

HALINKA: Like my dress? [*Sliding away*] I'm wearing it for the beauty contest at the Brittania tonight. They're supposed to have a marvelous orchestra. I know the trumpet player, he's a very good friend of mine, he said he'd arrange for me to sing.

STEFAN [*in a drugged voice*]: That's nice.

HALINKA: I'm not sure I'll go. It's so stupid, I hate it the way you parade around, and they look at you, like you're a . . . prize animal or something.

[STEFAN *moves close again, reaching out to kiss her neck.*]

It's supposed to be the prettiest night club in the Ghetto. [*She backs away,* STEFAN *following her.*] They've got these colored lights shining on the dance floor. I haven't danced in ages, I'm dying to—[*Abruptly, stopping him*] Say something. Talk to me. Men never talk to me. Say something!

STEFAN [*swallows*]: I think I'm getting a cold.

HALINKA: Oh, my god . . .

STEFAN [*reaching for her*]: Halinka . . .

HALINKA [*with fury*]: Just for once in my life I'd like to meet a man who doesn't treat me like—[*Suddenly she is weeping.*]

[STEFAN *watches her, baffled.*]

I'm sorry. [*Managing a wan smile*] I do like your uniform. [*Softly*] Do you love me?

[STEFAN'S *arms close around her, and they kiss.*]

RACHEL'S VOICE [*from inside*]: Halinka!

[STEFAN *and* HALINKA *separate.*]

Please, can you come and help?

STEFAN: I have to go, it's late. Are you . . . all right?

[HALINKA *nods, showing him a drained smile.* STEFAN *exits the apartment.*]

RACHEL'S VOICE: Halinka . . . [*She enters, her arms piled with furs.*] Quick . . . they're slipping.

[HALINKA *takes some of the furs from her. They*

pile them on the table. HALINKA *extricates a white jacket, and swings it over her shoulders.*]

HALINKA: My sweet little jacket.

RACHEL [*finding a stringy neckpiece*]: My monkey tail. [*She puts it around her neck.*]

[*A knock at the door.* HALINKA *opens it, revealing* BERSON. *He carries his concertina.*]

HALINKA [*haughtily*]: Yes, my dear man, what can I do for you? Baron Berson! Darling Baron! Allow me to present my sister—Countess Kuchloeffel. [*With a flourish,* RACHEL *flings her anemic furpiece across her shoulder.* BERSON *crosses to her, playing the elegant Baron.*]

BERSON [*clicking his heels*]: Enchanted.

[RACHEL *imperiously holds out her hand, and* BERSON *kisses it, continuing up her arm.*]

RACHEL: Ah, you devil!

HALINKA: You're just in time for the fashion show. The last night we have our furs.

BERSON: When do they have to be turned in?

RACHEL: Tomorrow.

BERSON [*lifting* RACHEL'S *neckpiece*]: I can just see the heroic stormtroops advancing on Moscow in this.

HALINKA [*tenderly caressing the fur against her cheek*]: Good-by, my baby.

[BERSON *tries on astrakhan hat and does a solemn kazatsky.* RACHEL *and* HALINKA *laugh, clap time, and shout yips of encouragement.*]

[PAN APT *enters.*]

PAN APT: Is that you, Berson? Rachel, have you seen my hat with the earlaps? [*As* RACHEL *and* HALINKA *exit to look for it, he draws* BERSON *aside.*] Well? Have you brought them?

[BERSON *produces an envelope and hands it over.*]

[PAN APT *glances through contents.*] Excellent, excellent. Good boy. [*He takes money out of his pocket and presses it into* BERSON*'s hand.*] Regard this as a little present from a grateful man. You've earned it. [*Turning, as* RACHEL *and* HALINKA *re-enter*] Did you find my hat? Everything is upside-down. It's impossible to find anything in this madhouse. [*He exits.*]

HALINKA: All we needed in here was Rutka and the rabbi.

RACHEL: They moved in with us this morning. So many people wandering the streets. It isn't fair for one family to take up a whole apartment. I think you and Symka ought to consider coming in, too.

HALINKA: Sure, join the parade.

BERSON: Seven, eight . . . nine of us in three rooms?

RACHEL: There are plenty living fifteen in one room.

BERSON: You want me in here?

RACHEL: My personal feelings have nothing to do with it.

BERSON: All right, I'll talk to Symka.

[RUTKA *enters, carrying a cloth coat lined with lambskin, and a fox jacket.*]

RUTKA [*dumps furs on table*]: You know, it's a good sign, the Germans taking our furs. The first evidence we've had that they're also suffering.

RACHEL: The Germans are shivering in Russia? Couldn't we make it worse for them? Maybe mutilate the furs some way so they can't use them. There must be a way.

BERSON: Simple. [*He takes her furpiece, examining it.*] Here, I'll show you. [*Produces penknife*] Just take out the lining. [*He cuts threads and rips away lining.*] Right here on the back, take a razor and cut little slits every two or three inches. Slits this way, slits that way. Almost all the way through, but not quite. And be careful not to cut the threads where the skins are pieced together. Then stitch back the lining. From the outside they look perfect—

RACHEL: But in the factory, when they start to put it inside some German officer's coat—

BERSON: It falls to bits.

RACHEL: Brilliant!

BENSON: I also imitate birds.

HALINKA: I'll get Mordecai's razor. [*She exits.*]

[REB MAZUR *enters.*]

REB MAZUR: Rachel, Rutka, listen! Berson, you too. The Russians just won a big victory at Kiev. Just now in the street I heard the Americans dropped bombs on Berlin! And—[*Realizes there has been no reaction.*] What? It's not . . . possible? No, eh? [*Deflated, he sits.*]

RUTKA [*consoling*]: It's all right, Papa. It doesn't matter.

[PAN APT *enters, carrying a suitcase and overshoes. He sets down the suitcase, and begins to don his overshoes.* REB MAZUR *crosses to him. He coughs.* PAN APT *hastily covers his face with a protective hand.*]

REB MAZUR: It's all right, it's all right, it's not a sickness.

PAN APT: It's not a wellness, either.

REB MAZUR: A suitcase?

PAN APT: A few old clothes I'm taking down to sell. Rachel, help me find my hat. [PAN APT *bustles around.* REB MAZUR *watches him like a hawk.*]

REB MAZUR: So it's true, eh?

PAN APT: Pardon me, I have an appointment.

REB MAZUR: The first time in my life I heard a rumor, and I wouldn't believe it.

RACHEL: What is he talking about?

PAN APT [*getting his overcoat*]: How should I know? Nothing. He's an old man. Bibble-bibble.

RACHEL [*to* REB MAZUR]: What are you talking about?

REB MAZUR: Ask him.

PAN APT: Ask me? What did they ever ask me, my children? For them I don't exist.

[MORDECAI *enters.*]

MORDECAI: What's happening? Where are you going?

PAN APT [*wheeling on him*]: I'm like a stranger. You pass me by and look right through me. I'm a monster, right? Yes, I pay bribes, I try to arrange matters. Does that make me a monster? Eh? Yes. I am leaving the Ghetto.

RACHEL: Leaving?

PAN APT: A monster. [*He spits.*] Yes! Leaving, leaving, to the other side! In ten minutes I will be a Pole! [*He feverishly yanks documents out of his pocket.*] Identity card, registration card, labor card. [*A little mirthless laugh*] Oh, they were not cheap, I'll grant you. The price of becoming an Aryan has gone up, like everything else. Eighteen thousand zlotys—one half in American dollars! But foolproof, absolutely foolproof! [*He starts to struggle into his coat. To* MORDECAI] Why are you staring? I'm nothing to you.

REB MAZUR: You think your religion is something you can take off like an overcoat?

PAN APT: I don't have to take off what I've never

worn. I'm a practical man, Rabbi. I've never had any use for religion. I never asked to be a Jew. It was wished on me!

REB MAZUR: The sign of the Jewish faith is on your body.

PAN APT: You'd be surprised what a plastic surgeon can do!

REB MAZUR: And the doctor also made you a new heart?

[*In answer,* PAN APT *rips the Star of David band off his sleeve.*]

PAN APT [*in a rush*]: Good-by, Rachel. Take care of David. Good-by, Mordecai. [*As* MORDECAI *turns away*] Yes, your back, turn your back on me! I remember once in the other house, the big house, years ago, we were all in the living room. Mama was reading to you. And you suddenly got up and came across the room and kissed me, and then went back without saying a word. It was just one of those . . . one of those surprises children give you. [*To* BERSON] It was nothing to him, an impulse. I've always remembered it. He was no more than seven . . . maybe six . . . [*He looks at* MORDECAI, *then fishes in his pocket.*] Here . . . a few stones I managed to put aside from the store. [*Forcing them into* MORDECAI*'s hand*] Take them. Take them!

[HALINKA *enters.*]

RACHEL: Papa . . . [*She embraces* PAN APT.]

[RACHEL *is holding him so tightly that he must tear himself away. He goes to* HALINKA, *crushing her to him.*]

RACHEL [*a bitter cry*]: Go if you're going! Go!

HALINKA: What is it? Where are you off to at this hour?

[PAN APT *has turned away, snatching up his suitcase.* HALINKA *looks around puzzledly.* RACHEL *is fighting not to weep.*]

Where is he going?

[PAN APT *exits.*]

[*As she begins to realize*] To the other side? Out of the Ghetto? *Papa!* [*She runs to the door, frantically struggling to open it.*] Papa, take me! Papa, please! [*She wrenches open the door.*]

[BERSON *crosses, stopping her.*]

Papa, my God, don't leave me here! Take me with you, I don't look Jewish, look at my face, you can take me!

[DAVID *comes in, confusedly trying to make out what is going on.* MORDECAI *closes the door.*]

[HALINKA *sobs.*] Don't leave me, Papa, take me with you! Papa . . . [*She slumps into a chair, weeping brokenly.*]

RACHEL: Let's have some music. Dolek, play something!

BERSON: What?

RACHEL: Anything!

[BERSON *takes up his concertina.* MORDECAI *becomes aware of the little bag of gems in his hand and, with sudden revulsion, flings them away.*]

[RACHEL *catches* DAVID *to her, holding him fiercely.*]

[RUTKA *slips out of her chair and touches* MORDECAI'S *arm.*]

RUTKA: Mordecai . . .

[MORDECAI *jerks away from her.*]

BERSON: I think I will play some German music. There's a decree, did you know, forbidding Jews to play Aryan music? I feel in the mood for a little defiance. [*He starts to play softly—Bach's "Jesu, Joy of Man's Desiring."*]

RUTKA: Mordecai . . . I'll tell you a secret.

MORDECAI: What is it?

RUTKA: I would like to marry you.

[MORDECAI *turns to her, unbelieving.* RUTKA *lifts her arms to him, and they embrace.* BERSON *plays.*]

[*Lights fade out.*]

[SCENE 6]

The street. Evening, a week later.

A trio of BEGGAR CHILDREN *led by a* RAGGED MAN *cross the street—the* CHILDREN *singing, the* RAGGED MAN *looking hopefully for offerings from the windows.*

BEGGAR CHILDREN [*in front of house, right*]:

Mama, Mama told me,
Please be sweet,
And you can have anything,
Anything to eat.

Don't you cry, don't you cry,
If you're hungry,
Eat a bit of sky.

Mama, Mama said to me,
Bread costs money,
Sky is free.

[*Crossing up to bakery*]

Mama, Mama told me,
Show a little joy,
And you can have anything,
For a new toy . . .

RAGGED MAN [*calling reproachfully*]: Good people, please! Please!

[*Above, a woman looks out, then disappears.*]

BEGGAR CHILDREN [*singing*]:

Don't complain, don't complain,
If you want a toy,
Play with the rain . . .

[*The woman drops a coin to the* RAGGED MAN, *who skillfully catches it in his hat, then leads the* CHILDREN *off, left.*]

BEGGAR CHILDREN [*exiting*]:

Mama, Mama said to me,
Toys cost money,
Rain is free . . .

[*Lights come up in the* APT *apartment. Candles burn in a seven-branched candelabra, and* MORDECAI *and* RUTKA *stand before* REB MAZUR. *Grouped around them are the wedding guests:* RACHEL, DAVID, HALINKA, MENKES, BERSON. *Only* SYMKA *sits, looking ill and wasted.*]

REB MAZUR [*chants, his voice breaking in formalized passion*]: *Boruch, atoh Adonai, elohainu melech ho'olum, a'sher kidushonu b'mitz vo'sov.* Blessed art Thou, O Lord our God,

King of the universe, Who has sanctified us by Thy commandments. Blessed art Thou, O Lord, Who sanctifiest Thy people Israel by the sacred covenant of wedlock. [*To* MORDECAI] Have you the ring?

MORDECAI [*slipping the ring on* RUTKA'S *finger*]: *Haray ot me'kudesh esli.* Behold, thou art consecrated unto me by this ring, according to the law of Moses and of Israel.

REB MAZUR: *Boruch atoh Adonai, elohainu melech ho'olum, boray pree ha'goffen.* [*Handing wine goblet to* RUTKA] Blessed art Thou, O Lord our God, King of the universe, Who createst the fruit of the vine.

[RUTKA *raises the goblet. From somewhere outside, the shrill blast of a police whistle is heard.* RUTKA'S *hand trembles.*]

SYMKA: What was that?

[*The guests turn their heads toward the window, shifting uneasily.* REB MAZUR *clasps* RUTKA'S *hand, firmly helping her drink. Then he passes the goblet to* MORDECAI.]

REB MAZUR: Blessed art Thou, O Lord our God, King of the universe, Who has created joy and gladness, bridegroom and bride, mirth and exultation, pleasure and delight, love and brotherhood, peace and fellowship. Soon there may be heard—

[*During the last words, outside there is the*

thudding of some heavy object against wood . . . the tinkle of broken glass. RACHEL *protectively puts her arm around* DAVID. SYMKA *clutches at* BERSON'S *arm. He pats her reassuringly, then disengages himself, goes to the window, looks out, comes back.* RACHEL *glances inquiringly at him. He shakes his head: nothing.*]

[REB MAZUR *continues in a steady voice, seeking to ride over the disturbance.*] Soon there may be heard in the cities of Judah and in the streets of Jerusalem the voice of the bridegroom and the bride—

[*Off stage, the police whistle shrieks again.*]

—the jubilant voice of youths from their feasts of song. Blessed art Thou, O Lord, who makest the bridegroom to rejoice with the bride. [REB MAZUR *hands a glass to* MORDECAI, *who puts it on the floor and stamps, shattering it.*]

BERSON: *Mazel tov!*

[DAVID *and* MENKES *break for the window.* BERSON *catches* DAVID, *and blocks off* MENKES.]

It's a raid, down on the next block. It's finished. Relax.

SYMKA: Oich, my heart is pounding like a drum. What are they doing down there?

BERSON: One a night, that's how they do it. So, for tonight it's over. Relax.

RACHEL: I have to go in the kitchen.

MENKES: You would think there was something to cook.

RACHEL: Maybe there is.

REB MAZUR: A feast.

MENKES: What?

RACHEL: You'll see.

REB MAZUR: Smell? You can smell it.

MENKES [*sniffs disbelievingly*]: Meat?

RACHEL: Meat.

MENKES: What kind of meat?

REB MAZUR: I'll give you a hint. Yesterday our feast was going clop-clop-clop down Franziskanska Street.

MENKES: A horse?

RACHEL: Clop-clop-clop-clop.

MORDECAI: We wanted to be married last week, but Rachel wouldn't let us. We had to wait until the horse died.

DAVID [*to* RACHEL]: Where did we get it?

RACHEL: Berson.

[BERSON *bows, acknowledging his modest triumph.*]

MENKES: People say you're working with a group—smugglers—what are they called?

DAVID [*proudly*]: The Wall Men.

MENKES: They say for a price you can get anything.

REB MAZUR: Blintzes and sour cream?

BERSON: We can get it for you.

MENKES: But a horse—it must have cost a fortune.

RACHEL: Ten thousand zlotys.

MENKES: How did you pay for it?

[RACHEL *looks at* MORDECAI. MENKES *turns slowly to him.*]

MORDECAI [*finally, low*]: With the jewels Papa left us.

[*An awkward pause.*]

MENKES [*seeking to cover the awkwardness. To* REB MAZUR]: It's allowed, for a Jew to eat a horse?

REB MAZUR: By the strict letter of the law, it is absolutely forbidden to eat a horse. [*Adopting a Talmudic singsong*] But when I began to reason, I reasoned like this. What is the basis of the law? The basis of the law is common sense. If we are hungry, what makes better sense than that we should eat?

BERSON: Bravo!

REB MAZUR: Also . . . the sixth commandment says: "Thou shalt not kill." If we allow ourselves to die of starvation, we are violating the law! *Therefore,* according to God's will, we should eat the horse!

[*All applaud.*]

[*Outside, a police whistle shrills again. Several sharp shouts, and a gabble of protesting voices.*]

BERSON: Halinka, sing us something.

HALINKA: How can I, with all that going—

BERSON: Sing! [*He takes up his concertina and plays the opening phrase of* "Dort'n, Dort'n."]

HALINKA: I can't.

REB MAZUR: Sing, *ketzele* . . .

[*Outside, the sporadic sounds of the raid continue at intervals.*]

HALINKA [*forcing herself to start, in a surprisingly pure and simple voice, a bit shaky at first*]:

"*Oy, dort'n, dort'n, ibern vasserl,*
Oy, dort'n, dort'n, ibern brink,
Fartribn hostu mich, in die vaytene lender,
Un denken, denk ich noch dir tzurick.
Oy, helf mir gotenyu . . ."

[*She breaks off in fright as the door bangs open —and* STEFAN *enters.*]

STEFAN: Sorry I'm late. I was on duty.

MENKES: What's going on outside?

MORDECAI: We heard the shouting, what was it?

STEFAN: Mordecai . . . *mazel tov!* [*Turning to embrace* REB MAZUR] Papa, *mazel tov*. Rutka . . . [*He kisses her and offers a package.*] Wedding present.

RUTKA: Oh, Stefan, what? What is it?

[*The* OTHERS *crowd in.* RACHEL *and* BERSON *stay with* STEFAN.]

BERSON: What's going on?

STEFAN: I've been out for the last three hours, rounding up people for the labor camps.

RACHEL [*shocked*]: You've been *what?*

STEFAN: They promised us we wouldn't have to . . .

[*He catches at* RACHEL'S *arm. She pushes him away, looking at him with disgust.*]

They promised!

RUTKA [*revealing the gift*]: A music box! Oh, I love them!

STEFAN [*to* BERSON *and* RACHEL]: Like dog catchers rounding up stray dogs. Pulling Jews out of chimneys, closets . . . garbage pails . . . It's not just one raid a night any more. They're going wild.

[RUTKA *has started the music box. It tinkles cheerfully.*]

[*Outside, there is a sharp whistle, and the measured krrop-krrop-krrop of marching boots.*]

STEFAN: I have to go. They'll notice I'm missing.

[HALINKA *sees him start for the door and catches his arm.*]

I have to go!

[STEFAN *hurriedly exits. The sound of marching boots is louder now. Everyone is listening, their faces mirroring fear and an edge of panic.*]

BERSON: Come, everybody, *mitzvah tanzen!* [*Outside, the boots thud.* HALINKA *starts for the window, but* BERSON *turns her aside.*]

RACHEL: *Mitzvah tanzen!*

[REB MAZUR *crosses toward the window.* BERSON *intercepts him, holding up the concertina, start-*

ing to play a grave, sweet Chassidic wedding dance, silently urging the rabbi to start.

Finally, REB MAZUR *turns slowly. He begins a measured clapping, turning to the others, encouraging them to join.* RACHEL *takes up the clapping; then, one by one, the others pick it up —except* RUTKA. MORDECAI *urges her with his clapping hands, but she simply cannot.*

Outside, screams are heard, and the confusion of terrified voices, the insistent police whistle. RUTKA *makes a sudden break toward the window, but* REB MAZUR *steps in front of her. His handkerchief is out. He dangles it invitingly. At last* RUTKA *takes the other end of the handkerchief, and they begin the slow, stately, gentle dance.*

Outside, the screams and shouts continue—a tragic counterpoint to the concertina.

RUTKA *breaks away from* REB MAZUR *and starts for the window again, but* RACHEL *catches her arm.* BERSON *livens the beat of the music to a hora tempo.* MORDECAI, DAVID, *and* HALINKA *join arms with* RACHEL *and* RUTKA, *forming a circle, whirling in the dance.*

Outside, the sounds of the raid rise in a crescendo of terror.]

CURTAIN

ACT II

«»

[SCENE 1]

SHPUNT'S *voice is heard singing:*

"Should I be a baker?
I don't have any bread;
Should I be a tailor,
I don't have any thread . . ."

Lights come up, revealing the street in summer. Six months have passed, bringing a swift and visible corrosion. Clothes have grown shabby; faces have grown gaunt.

Only the linden tree seems stubbornly to be living by the old calendar. Its summer foliage is full and green, its trunk enclosed by a bench where three Jews sit sunning themselves. One of these is a tiny sparrow of a WOMAN IN A BABUSHKA.

A man has entered. SHPUNT *captures him by the arm.*

SHPUNT: Come, Pinchek. The last tree in the Ghetto. Sit for a whole hour under the tree: all it costs you is two zlotys. Come, I've got a place for you. [*Pulls him toward the tree, singing*]

"I will go where the green trees grow,
And the little birds dance in the sky!"

[*To* WOMAN IN A BABUSHKA] Push over a little.

WOMAN IN A BABUSHKA [*not budging*]: Has the nerve to charge for sitting under God's tree.

SHPUNT: God made the tree: did God also make the bench? [*Grabbing man's arm*] Sit, enjoy yourself. [*To* WOMAN IN A BABUSHKA] Push over a little. Make room.

WOMAN IN A BABUSHKA [*ignoring him*]: You know what was my greatest pleasure in the old days? My greatest pleasure was a cup of coffee. I made—

SHPUNT: Push over! [*He wedges in, squirming to open a space, then rises to seat the man, but before he can do so, the* WOMAN IN A BABUSHKA *swiftly edges back.*] You rented a seat, lady, not the whole bench.

WOMAN IN A BABUSHKA: Some seat. Look, look, I'm not even getting shade.

SHPUNT: What do you want for two zlotys, the Vienna Woods? Please, don't aggravate me, I'm not a well man.

LOUD-SPEAKER: Attention! Attention! By order of the German authorities, all Jewish inhabitants of Warsaw will be resettled in the east, where labor will be provided.

[*A few people hurry in to listen. Every face is turned toward the* LOUD-SPEAKER. The WOMAN IN A BABUSHKA *rises, catching* SHPUNT'S *arm inquiringly, but he silences her with a gesture.*]

The following categories are exempt from resettlement: members of the Jewish Community Council and their wives and families. Members of the Jewish police. All those working in shops and factories owned by citizens of the Third Reich.

[*The people in the street start to hurry off.*]

WOMAN IN A BABUSHKA: What? What is it saying?

SHPUNT: Take your seat, Grandma. You can have the whole bench. We're being sent to the east.

[*He starts off left, singing*]

"I will go where the green trees grow,
And the little birds dance in the sky . . ."

WOMAN IN A BABUSHKA [*after him*]: To the east? What east? [*Left alone in the street, she turns her bewildered, frightened face toward the loud-speaker.*]

[*The lights dim out.*]

[SCENE 2]

Two weeks later. Night.

Lights come up on the APT *apartment.*

Overcrowding has brought a certain disorder: piles of blankets, clothes hanging from an improvised rack.

BERSON *stands at the window, playing* "Dort'n, Dort'n" *on his concertina. On the floor, right,* DAVID *sits on his rumpled bedding. Wearing a robe and slippers,* SYMKA *stands before the mirror, arranging her wig.* REB MAZUR *sits reading.* BERSON *stops his playing. In the distance, a sound of trains is heard, the iron grind and squeal of cars being shunted on a siding.*

BERSON: Hear it? They're making up the train for the east. Every night . . .

SYMKA: Dolek . . . like it this way?

BERSON: Pretty.

SYMKA: I was going to take a brown one, but then I saw this and I couldn't resist. I always wanted to be a blonde. Do you think the color goes with my eyes?

BERSON [*nods*]: They seem to be collecting the aged and the outcasts, mostly. Beggars, cripples, garbage looters, homeless refugees. Six thousand a day.

SYMKA [*to* REB MAZUR]: Ever since I was a little girl, I've been dying for blonde hair.

DAVID: You get a free ration of bread and marmalade if you volunteer.

SYMKA: Marmalade?

DAVID: If you go by yourself, the Germans give marmalade.

SYMKA: The morning after we were married, we had marmalade and hot rolls for breakfast, remember, Dolek?

DOLEK: Yes, I remember.

SYMKA: Right after the ceremony we left on our honeymoon. When I went to the closet to get my coat, I saw the marks Papa made inside the door. [*To* DAVID] When I was a child, he used to make this mark each year to measure how much I had grown. [*To* RABBI] When I heard our old house was bombed in the siege, all I could think was, the marks are gone. I wanted to run around and write my name everywhere, on the walls, and on the trees. . . . [*To* DOLEK] I mean, that's not right, for everything to just disappear. There ought to be a mark.

[*The front door bursts open, and* HALINKA *enters, followed by* RACHEL.]

HALINKA [*crows triumphantly*]: I got one! I got one! [*She circles the room, bestowing kisses on* DAVID *and* SYMKA.] I got one! [*She kisses* BERSON *on the tip of his nose.*] I've got a job! We walked our feet off: we must have gone to a dozen places.

RACHEL: Since they announced you won't be deported if you're working for the Germans, there are mobs at every factory door.

HALINKA: Wild. People down on their knees, really, on their knees, kissing the foreman's shoes, pleading for work.

RACHEL: There must have been five hundred of us, waiting there for hours.

HALINKA: Finally the foreman comes out. He's got places for three. Five hundred of us, and he's got places for three! "You . . . you . . . you" Me! I could have kissed him! I almost burst into tears.

BERSON: Where is it?

HALINKA: The Toebbens plant—repairing army uniforms.

BERSON [*to* RACHEL]: And you?

RACHEL [*shakes her head*]: It doesn't matter. I'll find something.

HALINKA: Look—[*Producing a small can*] A can of red paint! I found it in the street market. [*To* SYMKA] We can do our fingernails.

SYMKA: Let me see.

RACHEL: I found something, too. A present for you, Rabbi. [*She produces a tin.*]

REB MAZUR: Shoe polish? For these shoes? Dear child, to polish these shoes would be like feeding chicken soup to a corpse.

RACHEL: Who said it's for your shoes? It's for your hair. You know as well as I do, at the selection they take the oldest ones first. You get this on, you'll look like Casanova. [*She turns.*] Where do you suppose they're really sending them on those trains?

[*The room stills. The question hangs in the air, at once innocent and deadly.*]

HALINKA: What do you mean?

SYMKA: They said where they're sending them. To work in factories on the Eastern front.

RACHEL: Those scarecrows we saw shuffling out through the gate—they're supposed to work in factories? Up north they've cleaned out the villages. They used to send them down here, but we don't seem to be getting refugees any more.

HALINKA: Please, I'm feeling wonderful, so don't start anything.

RACHEL: They pack them on the trains, and that's the last anybody ever hears of them.

HALINKA: Just don't start. I'm not in the mood.

REB MAZUR [*rising*]: What do you mean, "that's the last anybody ever hears of them"? They can't vanish off the face of the earth.

RACHEL: How many have they taken already, in a week?

DAVID: Forty-seven thousand.

BERSON: How do you know?

DAVID: I heard it from Sonia—the one with the lisp. Her father works at the Community Council. [*Lisps*] Forty-theven thouthand.

HALINKA: See? It's practically over. Stefan told me all they want is seventy thousand. He saw the order from the German command, that's all they want, seventy thousand. A few more days, it will be over.

[*Outside, the echo of the trains is heard.*]

SYMKA: If they're not going to factories, where are they going?

RACHEL [*to* DAVID]: Go brush your teeth.

SYMKA [*pressing*]: Where are they sending them?

DAVID: What is it, something you don't want me to hear? I probably heard it already.

RACHEL [*ruefully*]: Yes, I'm sure. What am I trying to do, protect your innocence? [*Turning to the others*] It's not just the villages they're cleaning out. Yesterday there was a report from Lublin. They told them the same story they're telling us —started pushing them on the trains. They took them to a factory, yes, a splendid factory—a factory for making people into ashes.

HALINKA: I don't believe it!

RACHEL: One of them escaped, a capmaker named Lipski, and managed to send us a warning.

BERSON: You saw him, this Lipski?

RACHEL: I saw the message.

HALINKA [*pouncing*]: But you didn't see him!

RACHEL: I saw the message!

HALINKA: A scrap of paper! Anybody can write anything! Here, give me—give me a piece of paper, I'll write you a message they're giving away diamond bracelets in Bialystok!

RACHEL: I'm just telling you what I—

HALINKA: Stefan would have heard about it at the police: he would have told us!

RACHEL: Would he?

SYMKA [*tremulously*]: How can you come saying such things? You hear some crazy story, why do you have to throw us into a panic?

HALINKA: Because she's jealous. [*To* RACHEL] Because they picked me, because I got the job!

RACHEL: No . . . oh, no, Halinka . . .

HALINKA: You've always been jealous! Because I was Papa's favorite!

REB MAZUR: It could be a forgery. Maybe the Gestapo . . . to frighten us . . . a joke . . .

HALINKA: *Jealous, jealous, jealous* of me all your *life!*

RACHEL [*quietly*]: Yes. That's true. And how foolish, what a waste. But, you know, it's funny. Something's happened, my baby. I'm not jealous any more. I'm just trying to tell you—

SYMKA: Stop it! I don't want to hear!

RACHEL: They loaded them on trains in Lublin, and took them to—

SYMKA: You have no right! Dolek, make her stop! [*Her voice edged with hysteria*] You want me to die, don't you? You want me to die! [*Thrusting her face into* RACHEL's] Do you think you will ever have him? You fool, I'm his wife, and I've never had him. He's like wind! [*Weeping, she rushes from the room.*]

[*Silence. The squeal of trains.*]

RACHEL: It's so hot. Look at me: my blouse is soaked with perspiration. What did she mean? Why should I? . . .

[MORDECAI *enters.*]

MORDECAI: What's all the screaming?

HALINKA: Madame Rachel just looked into her crystal ball and decided the world is coming to an end.

REB MAZUR: Rochele, think for a minute. Why should they exterminate us? It doesn't make

BERSON: Symka, where are you going?
SYMKA: To the train station. I want the marmalade.

ACT II: *Scene 2*

SHPUNT: To the east? You're sending me to the east? A sick man you send to the east?

ACT II: *Scene 3*

sense. We're working for them, no? Right here in the Ghetto, factories are making uniforms, gun holsters, knapsacks, God knows what.

MORDECAI: We're valuable property. If Hitler wants to make peace, he can use us to bargain with.

REB MAZUR: It doesn't make sense.

RACHEL: What makes sense? Come out in the streets and show me what makes sense! You heard about Frankenstein? A German soldier, a boy, can't be more than eighteen. Rosy cheeks, face like an angel. Walks the streets with a machine gun, shooting down people for no earthly reason. One day it's men with blue suits, the next day it's women with hats. Takes out a little notebook and keeps track of the numbers.

REB MAZUR: So it's one madman.

MORDECAI: All right, they're not civilized. But they're still human.

RACHEL: And we aren't! *We aren't*—can't you understand that? To them, killing one of us is like a butcher kills a chicken, without thinking twice!

REB MAZUR: If the chicken looked like a man, the butcher would think twice.

HALINKA: The whole idea is ridiculous!

RACHEL [*to* BERSON]: And you—you also think it's ridiculous? Dolek?

BERSON [*looks up from tinkering with his concer-*

tina, shrugging, smiling]: I think life is ridiculous.

RACHEL: You think what they said about Lublin is crazy, a bad joke, there's nothing to worry about? Do you?

BERSON: On the road in Switzerland I met a Hungarian who was convinced that the moon was made of pot cheese. And you know, in three days of arguing, I could never really prove it wasn't.

RACHEL [*with fury*]: Answer me! Stop playing the comedian! What are you, a sight-seer, a tourist from America, somebody with a free ticket to the performance? Stand there with that little boy's grin. What is that idiot grin, what? Did someone once tell you it was charming? When will you get it through your head, childhood is over!

BERSON [*softly—and still with a trace of a smile*]: Yes. It's over.

RACHEL [*turns away to the others*]: All right. What we need is a hiding place. Stocked with candles, food, blankets. Some place that can hold out for days, weeks—big enough for us all, if necessary. A cellar, an attic, a hole in the ground . . .

MORDECAI: A hole in the ground? Do you think I want my son to be born in a hole in the ground?

RACHEL: Your . . . son? Your—

MORDECAI: I'm going to be a Papa.

RACHEL: Oh, Mordecai . . . [*Flinging her arms*

around him] Mordecai, my darling, *mazel tov!* [HALINKA *yelps and hugs* MORDECAI *too. The sisters kiss each other.*]

HALINKA: Rutka! Rutka! [*She runs out.*]

RACHEL [*starts out, then stops*]: She feels all right? Milk! Where on God's earth will we get milk? [*She rushes inside.*]

MORDECAI [*to* REB MAZUR]: I'm sorry. I didn't mean to blurt it out like that. Rutka wanted to tell you first.

REB MAZUR: What does it matter? [*He takes* MORDECAI's *two hands.*] May he live, with God's help, to a hundred and twenty—

BERSON: And be fat and prosperous, with teeth like a tiger and hair like a Russian wolfhound. [*Crossing to them*] May his sins be beautiful, and may he grow up to break the hearts of all the girls in Warsaw [*Catches* REB MAZUR's *eye, and grins*] . . . with God's help.

REB MAZUR: They're having a wonderful time in there. I can hear my daughter crying. [*He exits.*]

MORDECAI: You'd think nobody ever had a baby before. There's nothing to worry about. Rutka's as strong as a horse. [*Nervously*] I keep telling her she should stay in bed, but she doesn't listen to me. [*He exits awkwardly.*]

DAVID: What's he so nervous about? What's he got

to do with it? I mean, the woman has it all by herself, doesn't she?

[BERSON *cocks a speculative eye at* DAVID, *then thrusts him gently but firmly back down on his bed.*]

[RACHEL *enters.*]

RACHEL [*tucks in* DAVID]: It's late. Go to sleep. [*She turns off the lamp, throwing that area of the room into shadow.*]

[*The sound of children's voices is heard outside, singing, "Mama, Mama told me, please be sweet . . ."*]

[BERSON *has crossed back to the window.*]

BERSON: Children out in the courtyard, begging. Business is bad . . . nobody seems to be throwing them anything.

[RACHEL *takes up her mattress, unrolling it on the floor, and starts to put on the sheets.* BERSON *tries to help, but her swift movements block him.*]

How is Rutka?

[RACHEL *ignores him, occupying herself with making up the bed.*]

[*Outside, the children sing.*]

Would you like some tea? [*He jerks his head toward the window.*] Listen to them. Starving children. They've become as familiar as the neighbors' laundry. Even death doesn't disturb us any more. Two years ago, if anyone had told me . . . What an amazing thing man is. He can bear the unbearable.

[RACHEL *has finished fixing her bed on the floor. As she starts out toward the kitchen,* BERSON *crosses to her.*]

Rachel . . .

[RACHEL *whirls and slaps his face.*]

What's that for?

RACHEL: For being a liar! For that lying smile! Because you knew that what I was trying to warn them wasn't ridiculous. Didn't you?

BERSON: Yes.

RACHEL: But you couldn't say it! [*Close to weeping*] You had to pretend, stand there grinning, turn it into a farce! Why couldn't you say it?

BERSON [*taking her in his arms*]: Because it is impossible to convince warm, healthy human beings that they are going to die. Even if I said I agreed with you, it wouldn't have made any difference.

RACHEL [*low*]: It would have made a difference to me.

[*Outside, the children sing in their pure, piping voices.*]

BERSON: Is there anything to eat in the house?

RACHEL [*drained*]: I don't know, a few potatoes, a loaf of bread.

BERSON: Throw them down a bit of bread.

[RACHEL *gets bread, goes to the window, and throws it down. Outside, the singing stops.*]

Listen. I spend a lot of time poking around. It also occurred to me that it might come in handy to have a hiding place. I think I know where we can make one.

RACHEL: Where?

BERSON: Menkes's bakery. Make an opening in the back of the oven, right through the bricks. Tunnel down, and hollow out a bunker under the ground.

RACHEL: Go in through the oven? How can Menkes bake?

BERSON: Why not? We're below. Heat and smoke rises.

RACHEL: It sounds fantastic.

BERSON: You want to live these days, you have to consider the fantastic. Especially if you happen to be like me, in the insurance business. Here—here's a little insurance policy we just got out. [*He shows a booklet, riffling the pages with a craftsman's pride.*] A Uruguayan passport for a gentleman who is, shall we say, weary of his Polish citizenship. Absolutely genuine. Signed and stamped. With a little luck, our friend will turn up one of these days as a distinguished citizen of Montevideo. Oh . . . while we're on the subject of insurance [*Taking out papers*] . . . I got you some forged work papers. It's a clumsy job, but it might get you by for a while.

RACHEL: Thank you. [*Pocketing papers*] Dolek . . . I'd like to try and . . . insure my brother, David . . . get him to the Aryan side. You think you could find a hiding place for a little Jewish boy nine years old?

BERSON [*regards her narrowly*]: I think I can offer you a choice of insurance. First possibility: place him with some Catholic nuns. Foolproof. No danger.

RACHEL: And the other . . . insurance?

BERSON: Nothing but danger. A group of children being taken by an underground route to Palestine. Warsaw to Budapest, Istanbul, Palestine. On foot. The Jews are peculiar. They call this ordeal *tiul*—a walk. Just out for a little walk.

RACHEL: I'll have to ask him which he chooses. But I'm sure he will want . . . the walk. How soon can you—

BERSON: I don't know. Meanwhile, we'll fix up the bakery. And for David, I'll try to arrange it.

RACHEL: You're fond of him, aren't you?

BERSON: Fond of him. Fond of the rabbi. Fond of you.

RACHEL: You're beginning to feel for people, and it bothers you? You remind me of a lady I know who was sick for so many years that when she began to get well she thought it was another sickness.

BERSON: You've changed.

RACHEL: Have I?

BERSON: How long have you been in the underground?

RACHEL: What underground?

BERSON: There's a package of illegal newspapers behind the pipes, under the sink—

RACHEL: What makes you think—

BERSON: I saw you slip them in there.

RACHEL: You see everything, don't you?

BERSON: I'm a nosy man. At least let me find you a decent place to put them. Maybe I could hollow out the leg of a table . . . How old are you?

RACHEL: Twenty-five.

BERSON: A wonderful age to do stupid things.

RACHEL: I wish you were with us.

BERSON: I am not a martyr.

RACHEL: You have a safe face, you can get outside, you could help.

BERSON: I have all I can do to help myself.

RACHEL: You could—

BERSON: Don't try to drag me in, please!

RACHEL: Berson, the lone wolf. How I hate that about you, that cheap pose. Commit yourself! Commit yourself, live! And if you're hurt, so you'll be hurt.

BERSON: Commit myself? To what? You think this underground will amount to anything? We've been spit on, beaten, kicked around for so long, we've forgotten what it's like to fight back!

RACHEL: So we'll learn again.

BERSON: You think these Jews will really commit themselves? Little Mother, if I could believe that—

RACHEL: I couldn't live if I didn't believe it!

[SYMKA *enters from the kitchen in her robe, but barefoot, crossing to the door.*]

BERSON: Symka, where are you going?

SYMKA: To the train station. I want the marmalade. [*Cracking into hysteria*] I couldn't find my shoes.

[BERSON *leads her gently to the couch.* RACHEL *turns away, and crosses to her sleeping brother.*]

RACHEL: David? [*She kisses him lightly.*]

[REB MAZUR *enters.*]

REB MAZUR [*cheerfully*]: They're trying to decide whether they want a boy or a girl. When they decide, they'll tell the baby. [*He sits.*] I must tell you, my dear adopted family, I have made up my mind to something. I have decided to bury my Torah. If anything happened to me, who would watch out for it?

RACHEL: Nothing is going to happen to you, Rebbe.

REB MAZUR: The question is, where would be the best place? The place I would like to see it buried is with Hitler. I understand he's not in such good health lately, he's been having fits.

BERSON: How can you go on having such faith? I watch you: it baffles me.

REB MAZUR: Am I afraid to die, is that what you mean? A man who says he is not afraid to die is a liar. *How* they will die—that is what bothers most of our people. They are trembling because they think they will die a humiliating death. It is nonsense to feel humiliated by the Nazis, because we are better than they are. Yes, I am calm—because I know that any faith based on love and respect will outlive any faith based upon murder. [*Pause.*] Now, about burying my Torah. Will you help me, Dolek?

BERSON: We'll find a place. [*To* RACHEL] Come. I want you to take a look at the bakery.

[BERSON *and* RACHEL *exit.*]

SYMKA [*rousing herself*]: Dolek?

REB MAZUR: He went on a little errand.

SYMKA: I haven't done anything all day, and I'm exhausted.

REB MAZUR: So sleep.

SYMKA: I can't, I'm too tired. [*She sighs, closing her eyes again.*]

[STEFAN *enters.*]

STEFAN: Father . . .

REB MAZUR: What brings you here at this hour of the night?

STEFAN [*glances at* SYMKA *and keeps his voice low*]: I wanted to talk to you.

REB MAZUR: What is it, son?

STEFAN [*restless and abstracted*]: Where is everybody?

REB MAZUR: Inside. What's the matter with you? Are you all right?

STEFAN: I'm half out of my mind. [*Looking at his father for the first time*] Papa . . . the Germans have given us a new order. Each policeman has to bring four people to the train station every day. Or else he has to go himself. [*Prowling restlessly again*] They keep threatening they'll take Halinka. . . . I thought by staying in the police I could . . .

REB MAZUR [*trying to comfort him*]: Wait, we found some potatoes. Rachel made soup; you'll have a little.

STEFAN [*a whisper*]: Papa . . . I was wondering whether you would go with me to the train station . . .

REB MAZUR [*pretending he hasn't heard*]: Berson brought us some rice. God knows where he got it—

STEFAN: Father . . .

REB MAZUR: It is not like your mama's soup in the old days, but—

STEFAN [*low and urgent*]: You will be taken anyway. They'll get you one of these days. You can save me by going a few days sooner.

[REB MAZUR *regards him—a long, wordless gaze of bitter compassion. Then he turns away.*]

SYMKA [*waking*]: Oh . . . Stefan.

STEFAN [*still whispering to his father*]: They'll take you anyway! I thought you would want to help me.

SYMKA: What is it?

REB MAZUR [*crossing to her. Straightening her pillow*]: Nothing. It's nothing, my dear. [*He exits into the kitchen.*]

SYMKA: My hair must look a sight.

[STEFAN *crosses to her, pulls the pillow out from behind her, bends over, slips one hand behind her back and the other beneath her legs.*]

[*Giggling coyly*] Stefan, what are you doing? Don't be silly. Really, what if Halinka should walk in?

[STEFAN *lifts her and starts toward the door.*]

Stefan, what are you doing? I'm a married woman. Put me down.

STEFAN: It's all right.

SYMKA [*flirtatiously*]: Stefan, really, you're impossible. Where are we going?

[STEFAN *exits with his fragile burden.*]

[*Lights dim out on the scene.*]

[SCENE 3]

In the darkness, the BEGGAR CHILDREN *singing. Lights come up on the street. Twilight, several days later.*

The three BEGGAR CHILDREN, *led by the* RAGGED MAN, *cross slowly from right to left.* REGINA KOGAN *is one of them.*

BEGGAR CHILDREN [*singing*]:

"Shain bin ich shain,
Shain is mein nomen,
Ret min mir shidichim foon samen rabbonim.
Rabbonishe toreh is doch zayar grois
Bin ich bei main namen
Alichteka rois.

A Shain maidele bin ich,

Roite zeke lech trog ich,
Gelt in di tashen,
Vine in di flasshen,
Millich in di krigillach
Kinder in di veegelach,
Schrein alle shain,
Shain bin ich shain.

Besser a melamed,
A fille a baiser—"

[*Off stage, the crack of a pistol shot. A groan.*]

[*The* BEGGAR CHILDREN *cower against the* RAGGED MAN.]

[*A young German* PRIVATE *enters from right, putting his gun back in its holster. He makes a notation in a little notebook. Then, noticing the* CHILDREN, *he smiles at them, crosses to rumple the boy's hair and offer each a sweet.*]

PRIVATE [*encouraging*]: Candy . . .

[*Off stage a whistle blast. The* PRIVATE *hurriedly exits, left. The* CHILDREN *run off. The* RAGGED MAN *looks around dazedly, then crosses to the garbage can in front of the bakery and climbs into it, crouching out of sight.*]

[*The overture of terror that precedes a house raid: whistles, the siren, the rasp of the loudspeaker. "Raus! Out! All Downstairs! Raus!"*]

[*From somewhere outside, searchlights criss-*

cross the buildings, like sinister, roving eyes.]

[*From right,* BERSON *runs on, leading* DAVID *across to the bakery.*]

BERSON: Menkes!

[MENKES *emerges.*]

[BERSON *hands* DAVID *up.*] Is your fire out?

[MENKES *takes* DAVID *and disappears inside the bakery.* BERSON *follows.*]

[*Off, a burst of machine-gun fire.*]

[RACHEL *enters from house, urging* REB MAZUR *toward the bakery. As they cross, the German* PRIVATE *enters, cutting them off.*]

PRIVATE: This way. Over there, with the others.

[RACHEL *and* REB MAZUR *join the huddled group brought in by the* SERGEANT: *including* MORDECAI, RUTKA, *the* WOMAN IN A BABUSHKA, *and several others.*]

[*The* PRIVATE *crosses to the garbage can, kicks it, and patiently, almost politely, hauls out the* RAGGED MAN.]

[*The attitude of the Germans is brisk, efficient, almost bored. They are professionals with a small, annoying, ordinary job to do. They have been doing it now for months.*]

SERGEANT: *Anstehen, anstehen!* Line up. Have your papers ready.

[*From left,* OBERSTURMFUEHRER *enters and joins* SERGEANT.]

O. S. FUEHRER [*To* PRIVATE]: Take a look at the bakery.

[*The* PRIVATE *crosses to the bakery and enters.*]

SERGEANT [*calling off*]: Let's have some light on these specimens!

[*A floodlight hits the faces of the group huddled down the steps.*]

SERGEANT [*saluting* O. S. FUEHRER]: Where do you want the ones for the trains?

O. S. FUEHRER [*pointing right*]: Over there.

[MENKES *is pushed out of the bakery, then* BERSON—*followed by the* PRIVATE. BERSON *crosses to stand next to* RACHEL.]

RACHEL [*low*]: What happened to the package you took?

BERSON: I delivered it.

[O. S. FUEHRER *and* SERGEANT *approach the line. The first before them is the* RAGGED MAN, *deaf and smiling vaguely.*]

SERGEANT: Papers?

[*The* RAGGED MAN *cups his ear.*]

Papers!

[*The* RAGGED MAN *nods, smiling dreamily.*]

O. S. FUEHRER: To the right.

SERGEANT: To the trains.

[*The* RAGGED MAN *starts in the wrong direction. A casual crack from the* O.S. FUEHRER'S *swagger stick sends him staggering back, to the right.*]

[*The next man comes forward, cowering in the searchlight, offering his papers.*]

O. S. FUEHRER [*glancing indifferently at the man's papers*]: Excused.

[*The man hurries off. The second man steps forward and offers his papers.*]

O. S. FUEHRER: Resettlement.

[*The second man nods wearily, and trudges off to the right.*]

[*A third man steps up, blinking in the glare of the light.*]

SERGEANT [*examining his papers*]: Brushmaker.

O. S. FUEHRER: Excused.

[*The third man has been so certain of being sent to the trains that he now turns to join the condemned.*]

SERGEANT [*whistles*]: Hey, brushmaker! Excused.

[*The third man stares at him, then darts away, exiting left.*]

[*The* WOMAN IN A BABUSHKA *is next in line. She begins a frantic primping, pulling up her soiled stockings, pushing back a curl of hair, rubbing her cheeks to bring color to them.*]

SERGEANT: Papers?

WOMAN IN A BABUSHKA [*clearly has no papers*]: I was promised a job tomorrow at the Toebbens shop—

SERGEANT: Papers?

WOMAN IN A BABUSHKA [*In a rush*]: I was promised a job tomorrow, I'm an experienced seamstress, they promised me a job. I heard the whistle, I didn't have a chance to put on any decent clothes, I must look a sight, probably look like an old woman, I'm sure you'd never believe I'm only twenty-nine. Imagine.

[O. S. FUEHRER *smiles.*]

If I had a little lipstick, you'd see the difference.

O. S. FUEHRER: Resettlement.

[*The* PRIVATE *takes hold of her. She claws and scratches, finally yanking free.*]

WOMAN IN A BABUSHKA [*on her knees*]: I was promised a job tomorrow, I'm young, I can work, experienced seamstress, I swear on my mother's head, they promised me a job!

[*The* PRIVATE *gets hold of her again, dragging her off like a sack of wheat to the group at the right. The* WOMAN IN A BABUSHKA *abruptly stops shouting and seems to shrink into herself, collapsing like a doll that has suddenly become unstuffed.*]

[MORDECAI *advances, raising his hand to block the fierce light, handing over his papers.*]

SERGEANT: Labor battalion.

O. S. FUEHRER: Excused.

[MORDECAI *moves a few paces left, and stands*

tense and waiting. RUTKA *advances. She is noticeably pregnant.*]

SERGEANT [*looking over her papers*]: His wife?

RUTKA: Yes.

O. S. FUEHRER: Excused.

[RUTKA *crosses to join* MORDECAI.]

[*From left,* STEFAN *enters, herding* PAN *and* PANI KOGAN. *The* KOGANS *carry the last of their meager belongings. She carries a teapot, a suitcase, and her daughter's doll.* PAN KOGAN *carries various parcels.*]

[*At the sight of* STEFAN, BERSON *lunges forward.* RACHEL *grabs his arm, holding him back.*]

BERSON: Stefan! [*His voice low and hard, a promise of vengeance.*] How are you today?

[STEFAN *edges away.* SERGEANT *and* O. S. FUEHRER *are busy conferring over the clipboard*]

[PANI KOGAN'S *suitcase suddenly spills open.*]

PAN KOGAN [*hisses*]: Clumsy! All you know is to make a mess! Pig, a real pig! What did I do, God should punish me with such a wife? Creature! Look at her!

[*The* SERGEANT *calls them up.*]

SERGEANT: Papers? [*As* PAN KOGAN *hands over his papers*] Are you together?

PAN KOGAN [*Pause.*] No.

O. S. FUEHRER [*handing back papers to* PAN KOGAN]: Excused.

[PAN KOGAN *starts away.* PANI KOGAN *moves to follow, but the* SERGEANT *stops her.*]

SERGEANT: Papers?

[PANI KOGAN *has none. She stands there dumbly.*]

O. S. FUEHRER: For you, resettlement.

[PANI KOGAN *turns and slowly crosses to join the condemned.* PAN KOGAN *looks toward his wife and then, with an unearthly little sob, lets his own papers flutter out of his hand, and trudges across to join his wife. She touches his arm in thanks. He stands stiffly, showing no affection or surrender.*]

[SERGEANT *motions the next woman forward. She carries a bird cage and a bundle of clothes.*]

O. S. FUEHRER [*glancing cursorily at her papers*]: Resettlement.

[*The woman sinks to her knees and tries to kiss the* SERGEANT'S *hand. He matter-of-factly slaps her face. The* PRIVATE *steps up and hustles her off to the right.*]

[*Now, out of the cluster remaining on the stairs, steps a figure that has so far gone unnoticed. A little girl of nine, one of the beggar children. She comes slowly up to the Germans.*]

O. S. FUEHRER: Resettlement.

[*The girl turns and trudges off to the right. At*

the last moment, she spies the RAGGED MAN *and runs to bury her head against him.*]

[REB MAZUR *has half started toward the girl. He is brought back by the* SERGEANT *whistling sharply between his teeth.*]

SERGEANT: Papers?

REB MAZUR: I have no papers.

SERGEANT: Rabbi?

REB MAZUR: Yes.

O. S. FUEHRER: Resettlement.

RACHEL [*a cry of protest escaping her*]: No!

MORDECAI: Herr Obersturmfuehrer, sir . . . that's my wife's father, I'm on the labor battalion, they said the immediate families wouldn't have to—

O. S. FUEHRER [*indicating* RUTKA]: There is your immediate family.

MORDECAI: My wife's father—

O. S. FUEHRER: You wish to accompany him, is that it?

RUTKA: You have no right!

O. S. FUEHRER: You were excused, no? Perhaps there was some mistake.

RUTKA: No, no! [*To* STEFAN] Stefan! Tell them they have no right!

[STEFAN'S *face is impassive. He looks at the German* PRIVATE, *then turns his back on his father.*]

REB MAZUR [*To* RUTKA *and* MORDECAI]: Go, children, go home.

RUTKA [*starting forward*]: Papa . . .

[*The* SERGEANT *flings her back at* MORDECAI.]

REB MAZUR: Try to send me an extra shirt to the train station. [*He smiles calmly, giving them a little wave. Then he turns to* STEFAN, *shaking his head slightly with sadness.*]

[RUTKA *collapses, and* MORDECAI *scoops her up and takes her into the house.*]

[MENKES *advances, blinking in the glare of the floodlight, handing his papers to the* SERGEANT.]

SERGEANT: Pavel Menkes. Baker.

O. S. FUEHRER: Excused.

[MENKES *hurries back up into the bakery.*]

[RACHEL *is gazing brokenheartedly at* REB MAZUR. *The* SERGEANT *whistles to call her up. She hands over her papers.*]

SERGEANT: Rachel Apt. Leather worker.

O. S. FUEHRER [*a brief look at* RACHEL'S *papers*]: Excused.

[RACHEL *takes back her papers and starts left.*]

Here, wait a minute. Let me look at those papers again. [*Taking back papers*] What is your occupation?

RACHEL [*forcing it out*]: Leather worker.

[*As* O. S. FUEHRER *and* SERGEANT *huddle over the papers, a misshapen figure is hurled forward by the German* PRIVATE. *It is* SHPUNT, *with a broom in his hand. He pulls himself together, shoulders the broom, and clicks his heels together in a travesty of a soldier.*]

SHPUNT: Shhhhpunt!

[O. S. FUEHRER *dismisses him with an unamused glance.*]

[SHPUNT *makes a pathetic attempt.*] Hello, *guten tag*, good afternoon, how do you do, *sholem aleichem* . . . [*Ignored, and sensing that something is dangerously wrong,* SHPUNT *tries his dance.*] Yum peedle die, yom doodle dee . . .

[*No reaction.* SHPUNT *jigs violently.*]

O. S. FUEHRER [*jerks his head*]: Resettlement.

SHPUNT [*weakly*]: Hello, *shalom, guten tag* . . . [*Understanding finally dawning.*] To the east? You're sending me to the east? A sick man you send to the east?

[*The* PRIVATE *starts to haul him away. Protesting,* SHPUNT *pulls free.*]

A man with spots before his eyes, dizzy spells, hot and cold flashes? Shame! Spots, spots! Wait, you'll suffer. My death will be on your head, you hear? Me you send to the east?

[*He is suddenly staring into the barrel of the* SERGEANT'S *pistol.* SHPUNT *runs down like a broken toy, and shambles right to join the others.*]

[*The* O. S. FUEHRER *looks at the papers in his hand, then unceremoniously hands them to* RACHEL.]

O. S. FUEHRER: Excused.

[RACHEL *goes a few paces left, then turns, watching, as* BERSON *steps forward. All during the examination of his papers,* BERSON'S *eyes never leave* STEFAN.]

SERGEANT: Berson, Dolek. Carpenter.

O. S. FUEHRER: Excused.

[*As* BERSON *joins* RACHEL]

All finished here?

[STEFAN *starts to cross left, but the* O. S. FUEHRER *stops him.*]

Next building.

[STEFAN *turns back—and finds himself face to face with his father. He drops his eyes, skirts the rabbi, and starts to help the German* PRIVATE *shove the condemned off, right.* STEFAN *and the* PRIVATE *pause, waiting at attention as the* SERGEANT *and* O. S. FUEHRER *come past, exiting right. Then they continue their roundup.*]

[RACHEL *crosses to embrace* REB MAZUR.]

[*The German* PRIVATE *comes back to yank* REB MAZUR *away from* RACHEL *and push him off, right.*]

[*Offstage, a sharp whistle can be heard, and the*

SERGEANT'S *voice bellowing: "Out! All Jews downstairs!"*]

RACHEL: The rabbi, it's my fault, I didn't get him to the bunker in time. . . .[*Breaking*] It's my fault he was—

BERSON: Sha! [*Raising her face*] It's nobody's fault. They're closing in. If I want to get David out, I'll have to do it now. Tonight.

RACHEL: So soon.

BERSON: I'll have to go and make arrangements. Get him ready. Nothing to carry, no bundles, not even an extra shirt. Wrap his feet in rags. He has to move without making a sound.

RACHEL: Yes.

BERSON: Blacken his face—you can use the shoe polish. And, Little Mother, you'd better get out of that apartment. Pack up and move into the bunker. You, Mordecai, Rutka—

RACHEL: And you.

BERSON: I'll be going out with David.

RACHEL: But when you come back.

BERSON [*pause*]: I'm not coming back. Why should I come back? I'm suffocating behind these walls! I can't breathe! I'd have gone before, except for Symka. What reason is there to stay now except to find Stefan and crack his skull. I'll find him, that bastard.

RACHEL: It's hard, without Symka?

BERSON: I was . . . very fond of her. But, God forgive me, I don't know if I ever loved her.

RACHEL: Don't worry about God. Forgive yourself.

BERSON: I am not a man who feels things deeply.

RACHEL: I don't believe you.

BERSON: Do you know, even as a child I never cried. What kind of a Jew is it that doesn't cry? A freak of nature.

RACHEL: I don't believe you.

BERSON: Love. What does it mean? When they come with the guns, I have seen a son beat his own mother. A mother throw her child out of the window, her own child that she bore inside her.

RACHEL: Why do you torture yourself?

BERSON: Before the war, in that so-called normal life, we made such a show of love. Husbands and wives, parents and children. Now look around you. The nature of the human animal. Children buy poison, and the mama and the papa thank them for their thoughtfulness. Commit yourself, eh? Look around you, and show me who commits himself.

RACHEL: Dolek. Dolek, listen. Are you listening? I love you.

BERSON: Don't.

RACHEL: Let me say it! You're going: what harm

can it do? Once in my life I should have the right to say it! [*softly*] Oh, you . . . if you knew how I love you.

BERSON [*tortured*]: Love. That holy word. Who says you have to love? What is it, bread? You need it to live?

RACHEL: Yes. [*Gazing at his anguished face*] Go. You should go. Go.

BERSON [*a struggle—then*]: Take everybody to the bunker. I'll come for David tonight.

RACHEL: Yes.

[BERSON *exits.* RACHEL *closes her eyes, leaning back against the linden tree. Behind her,* DAVID *emerges from the bakery, and comes down the steps.*]

DAVID: Rochele . . .

RACHEL [*opens her eyes, then rises and crosses to him*]: Are you all right?

DAVID: At first I was sort of scared. It's dark down there in the bunker. Then I found the candles.

RACHEL: Come, You have to get ready. [*She puts her arm around his shoulder.*]

DAVID: For what?

RACHEL: For a little walk.

[*Lights dim out on the scene.*]

[SCENE 4]

Inside the bakery. The following day.

A semicircle of delegates from the conflicting tangle of underground organizations. Among those present are KATZ *and* RUTKA, *who is taking notes on the proceedings.*

The chairman is RAPPAPORT, *gray-haired, leonine, and slightly pedantic, with a face as noble as an old coin.*

RAPPAPORT: Gentlemen, I think today we can open the agenda with something encouraging. This matter of post cards from friends and relatives who have been taken off in the deportations. I've sent someone out to collect some of them. There seems to be evidence that the Germans are keeping the promises they made about work in the east.

[RACHEL *enters.*]

Have you got them?

[RACHEL *nods.*]

So let's hear.

RACHEL [*reading from sheaf of post cards in her hand*]: "The work is quite hard, but we eat well. Better than the Ghetto. Join me. Ask for Camp Fourteen." Signed: "Your cousin, Moishe Katzen."

RAPPAPORT: They've started coming in, the last week, these cards. Postmarked from various places on the Russian border.

RACHEL [*reading another*]: "Here we get two hot meals a day. My back is bothering me, but I am much happier here. Come." Signed: "Nachum Freund."

[KATZ *takes the cards to examine.*]

RAPPAPORT: These cards are being shown around. Some of our best people are wavering, and want to report for deportation.

KATZ: It's a trick. You have to be blind not to see that.

RUTKA: Hirshel Freund says his brother always had trouble with his back.

KATZ: You really believe these are authentic?

RUTKA: Yes. [*Defensively*] *Yes!*

KATZ: Three days ago you told me you were sure they were forgeries.

RUTKA: I changed my mind.

KATZ: Since when? Since they took your father?

RUTKA [*a wounded whisper*]: God damn you.

KATZ: Can't you see what they're doing? With every dose of poison they feed us a teaspoon of hope.

RAPPAPORT: They assured us they wanted only seventy thousand.

KATZ: They've already taken more than a hundred and eighty thousand. Listen—

RAPPAPORT: We have an agenda, if you don't mind.

KATZ: Listen, I just—

RAPPAPORT: At the proper time.

KATZ: *Now!* [*To the others*] Five days ago a Jewish policeman came to me. He's assigned to help load the trains.

RAPPAPORT: What is the point?

KATZ: The point is, he memorized the numbers on a few boxcars and kept track of how long it took them to go to the east and come back. [*He has their attention now.*] The transport left at ten in the morning. And all three cars were back the same afternoon—empty.

RUTKA: I don't under—

KATZ: It takes a through express at least twenty hours to get to the Russian border. A load of

Jews could hardly be considered rush cargo. And yet it required only three hours for our Warsaw brothers to go to labor duty in the east.

[*Silence. The others absorb the implications.*]

Slonim!

[SLONIM *enters, wiping his face with his cap—a stiff, graceless man with dour features and a defensive air.*]

We managed to slip this man over the Wall to investigate. Tell them.

[SLONIM *wipes his nose on his sleeve.*]

SLONIM: Well, first thing I did when I got to the other side of the Wall was to look up this railroad switchman, a Pole, used to be an old Socialist.

RAPPAPORT: How did he receive you?

SLONIM: He didn't kiss me on both cheeks, if that's what you mean. But he told me what I wanted to know. Where to find the trains that are headed east. I hid out there where I could watch. About eleven in the morning I heard it coming. A slow freight.

RUTKA: How did you know it was the Ghetto train?

SLONIM: I could hear the singing.

RUTKA: Singing?

SLONIM: In Yiddish. Somebody singing: "I Believe in the Coming of the Messiah." The train passed and . . . turned off . . . southwest.

KATZ: And then?

SLONIM [*snuffles*]: I started out, walking the tracks Walked all day. At night I slept in the woods. Next day about noon I came to this little station. There was a side track that swung off. I asked this old man where it went. He says: "Where you been, brother? That's the track goes to the Jew camp."

RUTKA: Jew camp?

KATZ: It's a village, it has a name?

SLONIM: Yes, a village, just outside a village. Auschwitz.

[*A first thin curl of smoke begins to rise out of the shadows into the light that spots* SLONIM.]

RAPPAPORT: You saw the camp?

SLONIM [*shakes his head*]: Can't get near the place. I asked the Poles what happens there.

RUTKA: And?

SLONIM: Thousands of Jews go in. Nobody comes out. Only clothes.

KATZ: Clothes?

SLONIM: Clothes, freightcars full of clothing. Dresses, baby shoes, shirts, pants. Clothing.

[*More and more smoke is wreathing into the light.*]

KATZ: That's all?

SLONIM: People go in. Thousands. But they don't bring in food. And all day, rising above the trees,

RACHEL: It's so strange, walking on the ashes. Hard to believe that underneath somewhere, people may be breathing, talking, sleeping.

ACT II: *Scene 6*

BERSON: Do you know what day it is? Easter Sunday. The streets full of people coming from church in their best clothes. I walked behind a young couple, the girl was wearing a spray of lilies of the valley.

ACT II: *Scene 6*

you see smoke. And all night the sky is red from the chimneys . . . and this stink in the air . . .

[*A heavy cloud of smoke hangs above* SLONIM. *Silence. The lights slowly come up, and we can see that the smoke has been coming from the pipe that* RAPPAPORT *is puffing.*]

RAPPAPORT [*finally*]: Nu?

[*They cannot absorb what their ears have heard, and so they must reduce it to a point on the agenda.*]

[RAPPAPORT, *The eternal chairman*] I hereby propose that we form a committee to consider ways and means of investigating this information. After all, he did not actually see this so-called camp. . . .

MENKES: It can't be true. They wouldn't dare!

[*A disorderly gabble of interruption.*]

RAPPAPORT: We will put it to a vote.

RACHEL: I have no right to speak here, but I think we ought to—

RUTKA: What we need are more workshops. Show them how useful we are—

RAPPAPORT [*cutting her off*]: Perhaps we should see the German commander. Offer him a bribe to stop the deportations. The question is—

[RACHEL *is taut with anger and hatred. She slams her hand down on the table.*]

RACHEL: I have no right to speak here. I am only an

assistant delegate, as they call me. . . . Talk. Talk. What are we, this so-called underground? A congress of blabbermouths? A wind machine! A hundred and eighty thousand they've taken. Enough to populate a city. Do you understand what is happening? *They are burning!* While we drone our way through the agenda. Yes, permit me to put a point on that agenda. *Who is next?* You? You? Your wife? My sister? [*Low, gasping for breath, but with the intensity of a consumptive*] Thousands herded off to the Exchange Place every day, and the only one I heard resist was a little boy who went mad, and began to yell: "I want to shoot, I want to steal, I want to eat, I want to be a German!" Why are we all so quiet? The most gentle bird does not go to death without a scream. This will be an eternal mystery: why didn't we resist when they began to resettle us? We should have run out, set fire to everything in sight, torn down the Wall! Now we are disgraced in our own eyes. And our docility has earned us nothing. You think talk will save you? You think work will save you? Bribery? *We must defend ourselves.* If we are too weak to defend our lives, let us at least defend human honor. [*Suddenly embarrassed and confused, she sways exhaustedly.*] They have taken . . . taken. . . . It is time we presented them with the bill. We must—[*She breaks off, drained.*]

KATZ: We'll teach them, Jews can be rough.

RAPPAPORT: We wish to do all we can in co-operation with other elements in the Ghetto, to resist . . .

[*Impulsively,* KATZ *leans forward, reaching out his hand.* RAPPAPORT *takes it, and the two stand shaking hands with an almost imperceptible motion—truce at last between the lion and the wolf.* KATZ'S *face is inscrutable;* RAPPAPORT'S *features are working with emotion.*]

[*Everyone else is up.* RUTKA *kisses* RACHEL.]

RAPPAPORT [*stilling the celebration with a single word*]: *However!* [*When there is quiet*] However, I should make myself clear. You may have misunderstood. I intended an expression of sympathy and common interest. But we will not be able to join formally with the rest of you. [*His impressive façade seems to dissolve, something awkward and fumbling emerging.*] This is . . . our position. We must . . . work with our Polish comrades. We expect assistance . . . We . . . assistance from them in a very few days . . . I expect to . . . I hope there has not been a misunderstanding. I trust . . . [*He looks around, but obviously sees nothing, as his eyes are full of tears. He sits down with a jarring suddenness.]*

[The room is deathly still.]

KATZ [*curtly*]: It is time, nevertheless, to move. With or without. I have here a proposal for a single resistance organization. Strict military lines. I think we can muster six hundred fighters.

RUTKA: Where will we find the weapons?

KATZ: If we can't get guns, we'll use gasoline, knives, clubs, crowbars, our bare hands.

[RAPPAPORT *slowly rises.* RACHEL *reaches out, drawing him into the cluster that crouches around* KATZ.]

As a symbol of my own group's intention to pool our resources unstintingly, we wish to offer our entire arsenal to the Jewish Fighters Organization.

[Lights begin to dim.]

[*With a faint, wry smile,* KATZ *reaches into his pocket and pulls out a German Luger. He drops it with a clatter on the table.*]

[Lights black out.]

[In the darkness, the sound of the train is heard, and the piercing scream of its whistle—a cry from hell.]

[SCENE 5]

Sounds: the krrop, krrop, krrop of boots. The grating voice of the LOUD-SPEAKER *barking:* "*Alle 'raus. You will present yourselves at once for examination of documents.* Alle 'raus!"

Lights come up on the street. It is afternoon, the following spring.

Nothing stirs. The street is empty and silent. The LOUD-SPEAKER *barks.*

STEFAN *comes on leading* HALINKA *by the hand. They cross—then stop, staring off.*

A German PRIVATE *enters.* STEFAN *salutes;* HALINKA *smiles nervously. They start past, but the* PRIVATE *moves, blocking their way.*

. . .

STEFAN [*pointing to his cap*]: Police. It's me, remember? Officer Mazur.

[*The German* PRIVATE *still blocks their way.*]

Police.

PRIVATE: New regulation this morning. Police are no longer exempt from deportation.

STEFAN [*as though it had not penetrated*]: Police.

HALINKA: No! [*She starts to turn and run, but* STEFAN *catches her arm.*]

STEFAN: Police . . . It's a mistake. They promised us. Your Obersturmfuehrer himself gave us his word of honor we wouldn't be sent away. He promised!

PRIVATE [*shoving them*]: This way!

STEFAN [*struggling*]: No! He swore on his word of honor! He promised!

[*The* PRIVATE *pushes* STEFAN *and* HALINKA *off left.*]

He promised!

[*The street is empty now.*]

LOUD-SPEAKER [*addressing the empty street*]: You will present yourselves at once for examination of documents. All out! *Alle 'raus!* [*Silence.*] *Alle 'raus!*

[*German* SERGEANT *and* O. S. FUEHRER *enter.*]

[SERGEANT *blows a blast on his whistle. The street answers with silence.*]

[*German* PRIVATE *re-enters.*]

O. S. FUEHRER: They're in there, all right. They're in there.

[SERGEANT *blows his whistle.*]

Go and get them.

[PRIVATE *and* SERGEANT *cross to the apartment house and enter.*]

LOUD-SPEAKER: You will present yourselves at once for examination of documents. At once. All out!

[*Silence. Then, from inside the house come shouts, the sound of a scuffle.*]

[MORDECAI *is flung out of the doorway, landing on his hands and knees. His mouth is bleeding. He is followed by the* SERGEANT, *who drags him upright and shoves him forward.*]

[*From inside the house comes the sound of a shot. Then the* PRIVATE *appears in the doorway, sagging oddly, a strange look on his face.*]

PRIVATE [*disbelief*]: *Juden waffen* . . . The Jews have weapons. . . . [*A piercing cry.*] *The Jews Have Weapons!*

[*The* PRIVATE *starts to run.* RACHEL *appears on Mazur Balcony and fires at the* PRIVATE, *who pitches off the bakery bridge onto the street. The* SERGEANT *and* O. S. FUEHRER *flee, left.*]

LOUD-SPEAKER: You will present yourselves immediately for examination of documents! *Alle hinunter!*

[KATZ *bursts out of the house, carrying a pistol. He runs right, crouches against the wall of the bakery, and fires off, after the retreating Germans.*]

[*Behind him,* MENKES *and* RAPPAPORT *emerge from the house.*]

KATZ: They're running! Sweet God in heaven, look at them run!

[MENKES *spies the machine pistol dropped by the German* PRIVATE. *He scoops it up and tosses it to* KATZ.]

KATZ [*kissing the gun*]: Oh, you dove! Little sweetheart!

[*He hands his pistol to* MENKES, *gesturing upstage.*]

Up there.

[MENKES *darts upstage, looking off, keeping watch.* RUTKA *emerges from the house, crossing swiftly to* MORDECAI.]

RUTKA: Are you all right?

MORDECAI [*pointing to the dead German* PRIVATE]: Why did we wait so long?

[SLONIM'S *head pops out of the window of the* APT *apartment.* RACHEL *emerges from the house.*]

RACHEL [*embracing* KATZ]: Oh, it's good! Oh, God, how good it is!

[MENKES *comes back down to the street.*]

MENKES: All clear.

[RACHEL *surveys* MENKES, SLONIM, *and* RAPPAPORT, *shaking her head with wonder.*]

RACHEL: Look at you, look at you.

MENKES: What about it?

RACHEL: You look different.

RAPPAPORT: How, different?

RACHEL: I don't know. You don't look like victims, you look like men.

LOUD-SPEAKER: *Alle 'raus! 'Raus!* You will present yourselves immediately for examination of—

[*At the* LOUD-SPEAKER'S *first words,* RAPPAPORT *and* MENKES *race to the tree.* RAPPAPORT *silences the* LOUD-SPEAKER *abruptly by yanking out the wires.* MENKES *climbs the tree.* RACHEL, RUTKA, *and* MORDECAI *cross to watch, and* MENKES *starts to tug at the* LOUD-SPEAKER *horn. At each tug, they cheer him on—a rhythmic chant. The* LOUD-SPEAKER *finally comes loose, and* MENKES *flings it down.*]

MENKES [*throwing back his head—a victorious cock crow*]: COCK-A-YOU-YOUUU! [*Off right, a burst of gunfire.*]

KATZ: Ours! They've ambushed a German patrol, they're giving it to them good!

[RUTKA *and* MORDECAI *cross right. From his perch in the tree,* MENKES *sees something off, right.*]

MENKES: Katz! One of them over there, hiding in the doorway!

[KATZ *takes aim off right, and fires.*]

MENKES: *Mazel tov!*

[*Off right, a burst of machine-gun fire.*]

KATZ [*looking off right*]: Germans! They're coming back, with machine guns. Get down—take cover!

[*The others take cover, crouching against the house.*]

RUTKA [*pointing to* GERMAN PRIVATE]: Mordecai . . . his uniform. Get his uniform!

[MORDECAI *ducks across, and starts to strip the* GERMAN SOLDIER.]

[*From off right, the sound of heavier guns, and a clank of armored treads.*]

KATZ: Tanks . . . coming this way. Come on, everybody, into the bunker. Quick!

[RAPPAPORT, MORDECAI, RUTKA, *and the others cross swiftly and disappear into the bakery.* MENKES *starts to scramble down out of the tree.* KATZ *takes aim, fires, and then ducks into the bakery.* RACHEL *starts to follow him.*]

[*Off, the clank of the approaching tanks grows louder.*]

RACHEL [*from the bakery doorway*]: Menkes! Hurry!

MENKES: Yes, I'm coming.

[*From off, a staccato rip of machine-gun fire.*

MENKES *is hit and falls, his pistol skidding away.*] [RACHEL *runs to him.*] The pistol . . . Take the pistol. . . .

[*He dies.* RACHEL *frantically tries to drag him toward the bakery, but cannot.*]

[*The approach of the tank grows louder. Another burst of machine-gun fire.*]

[RACHEL *gives up, grabs* MENKES'S *pistol, and races into the bakery.*]

[*The sound of the tank roars toward the street, deserted of all but the two corpses.*]

[*Lights dim out on the scene.*]

[SCENE 6]

In the darkness, the ear-splitting sounds of a bombardment. As it fades, slowly, we become aware of:

The street. Twilight, almost three weeks later. A horizon reddened with the reflection of fire dimly lights the city outside the Ghetto, serene and untouched. As for the street: it is as though some great hand had passed over the landscape, leaving in its wake utter desolation. The apartment house is gone; the bakery is a gutted pile of rubble. The linden tree is a skeleton, a charred hieroglyphic signifying the death of the world. Nothing stands intact but the Wall.

There is a distant booming of artillery.

From right, into this lonely, smoking scene, prowls a small figure. It is REGINA KOGAN, *tattered, unkempt, a lost animal poking in the ruins. She stops, sensing danger.*

From off left, the sound of dogs is heard. Crouching, REGINA KOGAN *scuttles off.*

Beneath the ruins of the bakery, lights come up on the bunker. Its ceiling is shored with timbers, and there are two rough sleeping shelves, rear. An iron stove, a mattress laid on a few boxes, a small table with a cluster of empty bottles.

At rear, a tunnel exit, blocked by a wooden barricade door.

RUTKA *paces, cradling her baby.*

RUTKA [*humming* "Dort'n Dort'n"]: Shaa . . . shaaa. Aie, baby, do you have a life. Eat and sleep. Your mama should have such a life.

[*The baby is asleep. Gently,* RUTKA *sets him in a box on the lower bed. Hearing a sound in the tunnel, she freezes. She takes up a pistol and crosses to the door.*]

Who's there?

RACHEL'S VOICE [*from the tunnel*]: Amkho.

RUTKA: *Vos sugt der rebbe?*

RACHEL'S VOICE: *L'chaim!*

[RUTKA *unlocks the barricade, and* RACHEL *crawls in.*]

RUTKA: Rachel . . . are you all right?

[RACHEL *rises, nodding. She carries a pistol, wears a man's cap, and her shoes are wrapped in silencing rags.*]

And Mordecai?

RACHEL: He's coming.

[MORDECAI *crawls in.*]

Clean your gun.

MORDECAI: I'm hungry.

RACHEL: First clean your gun.

[MORDECAI *sits on stool and dismantles his pistol.*]

It's so strange, walking on the ashes. Hard to believe that underneath somewhere people may be breathing, talking, sleeping.

RUTKA: How many do you suppose are still left? A thousand? A hundred?

MORDECAI: We met six of them wandering in the smoke. Ghosts, shadows with bundles.

[*The baby whimpers.*]

RACHEL: Here, let me take him. [*Crossing to lift the baby in her arms*] Mole, little mole. Someday I'll take you out and show you the sky. Oi, will you be surprised. The sun I'll show you, and the moon, and all the sweet stars.

RUTKA: He needs something to eat, more than noodles and water.

MORDECAI: Who doesn't? Whew—it stinks in here.

RUTKA: You want fresh air? We'll send you for a holiday to the mountains.

MORDECAI: Believe me, if we ever get out this, I'll go to the mountains. Sit under a tree and eat. *Mamenyu,* will I eat! Chopped liver, with a little vodka, eh, just a sip to bring out the flavor, then a nice chicken soup—

RUTKA: Stop!

MORDECAI: Raisin strudel . . .

RUTKA [*surrendering*]: Beef goulash.

MORDECAI: Pickled herring!

RUTKA: Blintzes with sour cream! [*Pause.*]

RACHEL [*cradles the baby, crooning dreamily*]: Stuffed cabbage . . .

MORDECAI: I'll settle for an apple.

RACHEL: Mordecai—you hear? Someone in the tunnel.

[*With raised pistol,* MORDECAI *crosses to the door.* RACHEL *hands the baby back to* RUTKA, *and takes up her weapon.*]

KATZ'S VOICE [*from tunnel*]: It's me. Open up.

MORDECAI: *Vos sugt der rebbe?*

KATZ'S VOICE: *L'chaim.*

[MORDECAI *opens the barricade, admitting* KATZ.]

KATZ: I think there is another group still fighting, over in the brushmakers' district. I could hear the shooting, but I couldn't get through.

MORDECAI: Why do we keep hanging on? Believe me, Berson knew what he was doing when he got out. What's the honor in committing suicide?

RACHEL: There are people still living out there under those ruins.

MORDECAI: One by one the Germans are clearing out the bunkers.

KATZ: We can at least make it harder for them.

MORDECAI: For how long? Without food, for how long? We've been fighting for nineteen days. What have we proved?

RACHEL [*quietly*]: We've proved it is possible to resist, even in hell.

MORDECAI: I'm about finished. When I see a German, I tremble.

KATZ [*puts a comforting arm around* MORDECAI'S *shoulder*]: The first thing to do is go out and try and make contact again with the others.

MORDECAI: There's no more fighting organization, just scraps and pieces.

KATZ: Mordecai, stop looking for an excuse to run.

MORDECAI [*flaring*]: When I talk about getting out, must you always think of it as an act of cowardice? [*More gently*] I'm just worried about the baby.

KATZ [*making truce*]: I know. Come. We'll make a round of the bunkers. Try and find the others.

[*To* RACHEL] Is there any more gasoline?

[*She nods "yes."* KATZ *picks up a bottle, hands it to* MORDECAI.]

We'd better mix a few cocktails, in case we run into tanks.

RUTKA: I'll stand guard.

[MORDECAI *and* KATZ *exit left.* RUTKA *hands the baby to* RACHEL, *and exits into the tunnel.*]

RACHEL [*sits singing to the infant*]:

"Unter Yeedeles vigele
Shteyt a klor vice tsigele—"

[*She breaks off, as a concertina is heard softly playing the first phrase of* "Dort'n, Dort'n." RACHEL *listens, then wipes her eyes.* A *dream?*]

"Dos tsigele is geforen handlen,
Dod vet zine dine beruf,
Rozhenkes mit . . . mandlen—"

[*She breaks off again. The concertina is faintly playing the next phrase of* "Dort'n, Dort'n." RACHEL *swallows painfully, but cannot go on.*]

Is anyone thirsty? I'll portion out the water.

[RUTKA *appears from the tunnel.*]

RUTKA: We've got a visitor.

[*Behind her,* DOLEK BERSON *enters. He carries his concertina.*]

BERSON: It's not the easiest place to get to, this palace of yours. I couldn't find it in the telephone book.

[RACHEL *simply stares at him unbelieving.*]

RUTKA: He was wandering around up there, giving a concert.

BERSON: I couldn't locate the entrance. So I decided the thing to do was advertise myself, and let you come to me.

[*Hearing* BERSON'S *voice,* MORDECAI *enters from left.* RUTKA *takes the baby from* RACHEL.]

Mordecai . . .

MORDECAI [*stares*]: Berson! [*He puts out his hand.* BERSON *grabs it, and yanks him into a rough embrace.*]

[KATZ *enters. A poised moment, as he stares at* BERSON.]

BERSON: Katz . . .

KATZ [*finally*]: Hello, Dolek. [*A faint grin. He takes* BERSON'S *hand.*] Welcome home.

BERSON [*produces bottle*]: Vodka.

[MORDECAI *snatches it.* BERSON *digs in his pocket.*]

Loaf of bread.

[RUTKA *takes it, breaks off a chunk, and passes it around.*]

This morning's Warsaw newspaper.

[KATZ *grabs it.*]

If you're looking for the story about the Ghetto, it's on the last page.

[*Off, gunfire is heard more clearly.*]

KATZ: German Army communiqué. "The former Jewish District of Warsaw is no longer in existence."

[*As* RUTKA *passes out chunks of bread,* BERSON *crosses to* RACHEL.]

BERSON: Look. [*He offers a thin branch.*]

RACHEL: What is it?

BERSON: From the linden tree.

RACHEL: Our poor tree.

BERSON: I thought it was dead. Look, it's putting out buds again.

RACHEL: Rutka had her baby.

BERSON: A boy?

[RUTKA *shows* BERSON *the child.*]

RACHEL: Israel. The king of the bunker. You should hear him bellow when he's hungry.

BERSON: A one-man resistance movement.

RACHEL: Oh, Dolek, what a surprise we gave them. You should have heard them screaming: "*Juden waffen!* The Jews have weapons!"

KATZ: For two weeks we stopped them dead, tanks and all. They didn't dare to stick their noses in the Ghetto after twilight. Until they brought up the big guns and began to smash us flat.

MORDECAI [*as he opens the vodka*]: Nobody surrenders.

KATZ: They have to smoke us out. Blow up the bunkers with dynamite.

MORDECAI [*takes a sip of vodka, closing his eyes dreamily*]: Oh, God . . . [*He passes the bottle to* RUTKA.] Taste.

RUTKA [*starts to drink—pauses*]: To what?

BERSON: To the baby.

RUTKA: Israel. [*She drinks, and passes the bottle to* RACHEL.]

RACHEL: To the rabbi. [*She drinks, and passes the bottle to* KATZ.]

KATZ: *L'chaim!* [*He drinks, and passes the bottle to* BERSON.]

BERSON: *L'chaim.* To life. [*He drinks.*]

[*In the distance, the artillery fire rumbles faintly.*]

RACHEL [*to* BERSON]: And my brother, David?

BERSON: The last I heard, he had reached Budapest. My friends tell me he behaves like a grown man. I also managed to find your father. He's living in a stable across the river, sleeping in a horse's stall.

RACHEL: How is he?

BERSON: He and the horse have reached an understanding. He's thinking of going to Germany. He's heard it's quite easy for Poles to get work as domestic servants.

RACHEL: He asked about us? Tell me, you can tell me.

BERSON: Mostly he talked about Halinka.

[*This is painful for* RACHEL.]
He is reduced to combing horses in a broken-down stable, he sleeps in dung, and dreams of his little princess.

RACHEL: Halinka is dead. Stefan also. His policeman's uniform didn't save him.

BERSON: Menkes?

RACHEL: Gone. The first day of the fighting. We are dwindling, Dolek. So many dead under the ruins . . .

KATZ: How did you get in?

BERSON: There was a commotion on Bonifratarska Street. The Polish underground, I think, trying to create a diversion. Grenades dropping like chestnuts. I came over the Wall.

MORDECAI: Could we get out that way?

BERSON [*shakes his head*]: The district was already on fire when I came in. Outside the Wall, every fifty yards, a German with a machine gun.

MORDECAI: I understand there is a way out through the sewers.

BERSON: It's a nightmare. Take a wrong turn, you can wander around in circles for days. You can rot down there.

KATZ: We'll make a round of the bunkers. See who is left, consolidate our forces.

BERSON: I'll go with you.

KATZ: Two of us are enough. We should have a guard in the tunnel. Whose turn is it?

RUTKA: Mine. [*She puts the baby into his box crib and exits into the tunnel.*]

KATZ [*to* RACHEL]: We'll need ammunition. How much is left?

[RACHEL *shows him the box.* KATZ *scoops up some shells.*]

We'll take half. [*He exits into the tunnel, followed by* MORDECAI.]

[RACHEL *locks the barricade door, then turns back, pausing to stand and stare at* BERSON.]

RACHEL [*finally*]: The place is always in a mess. Impossible to keep it clean. [*She picks up the newspaper, then turns to look at* BERSON.] You came back. You came back. . . . Why?

BERSON: I was thinking of going north to a farmer I know, a quiet village. I had to make arrangements: it took time. Sometimes in the evening I would go and look at the river. The Vistula, calm and easy, making its way to the sea. I'd think: "Take a good look, my boy, that's the way to live."

RACHEL: I can see you, with that grin. Oh, how well I know you.

[*The sound of artillery is a bit louder now.*]

BERSON: Then the German army slammed into the

Ghetto. And you began to fight back. I could hear it, all hell breaking loose inside the Wall— and everyone out there pretending it was nothing, it wasn't happening. Those explosions, like all the animals roaring in some crazy zoo. Three days, seven days, ten, Christ, how long can they keep it up? I tried, I tried, *I tried* not to think about it!

[*In the distance, the sound of the artillery is faint, mingling now with the sound of the merry-go-round.*]

RACHEL: And you came back.

BERSON: This morning I started out to leave for the north. Do you know what day it is? Easter Sunday. The streets full of people coming from church in their best clothes. I walked behind a young couple. The girl was wearing a spray of lilies of the valley. The merry-go-round playing in Krasinski Park. And smoke slanting across the sky, the Ghetto burning.

[*Merry-go-round slowly begins to fade out, leaving only the rumble of artillery.*]

I walked along with the feeling that I . . . had not survived. I always thought that just to live was enough. To live *how?* To live *with whom?* In here—together—you were alive. And out there—alone—I was dead. I just kept walking along toward the smoke, thinking about you. . . . [*He begins to weep.*] "Idiot, you stupid idiot, what are you doing? Turn around, get out while there's still time!" I came past the corner of Bonifratarska, and saw the Wall—and that was when I knew I was coming back.

[*A sharp explosion of artillery. Then it fades down to fainter, intermittent firing, continuing during the following conversation.*]

RACHEL: Ah, Dolek . . .

BERSON: If we mean to go on, we'll need supplies. Ammunition, medicine—

RACHEL: Dolek . . .

BERSON: I'll have to find a way to get out again.

RACHEL [*low and urgent*]: Dolek . . .

BERSON: Get in touch with the Polish underground.

[*He turns to her entreaty, reaching out to touch her hair tenderly, wonderingly.*]

RACHEL: You . . . oh, you, with that face . . .

[*The sound of the artillery rises, as she kisses him with a consuming passion. Slowly his arms go around her, responding to her ardor.*]

[*Lights black out on the bunker.*]

[*A passage of time, marked by the sound of cannon fire.*]

[*Above, in the street, evening has come. A red glow burns in the sky.*]

[*Lights come up again in the bunker.* RACHEL *is*

lying on the floor with her head pillowed on BERSON'S *lap.*]

[*The artillery continues, distant now.*]

RACHEL: Dolek. Dolek, Dolek, Dolek . . .

BERSON: Do something. Anything, so I can watch you.

RACHEL: Tell me. What is your favorite color? What were you like as a little boy? Tell me, tell me! My darling, that's what love is, to be able to tell everything and know that you won't be laughed at and you won't be judged. I love you. [*She kisses him.*] What did you think when you first saw me?

BERSON [*a derogatory grunt*]: Ehh. A bad-tempered child playing mother.

RACHEL: Funny-looking?

BERSON: Funny-looking. [*Turning her face*] How queer. You've become a beauty.

RACHEL: Dolek, listen, I want to ask you something. Don't laugh at me. For making love, do I . . . have any talent?

BERSON: Yes. Quite a talent.

RACHEL: I always suspected. [*She smiles peacefully.*] Do you suppose I will have a child? Oh, I would like one.

BERSON: Are you in such a hurry to give birth to another child? Haven't you seen what can happen to children?

RACHEL: I'm surprised at you. That is exactly the reason. My darling, the only way to answer death is with more life.

[*There is a sound from the tunnel.*]

[*Annoyed*] Vos sugt der Rebbe? [*She gets up, crosses to the door, and admits* KATZ, MORDECAI, RAPPAPORT, *and* RUTKA.]

KATZ: We ran into a messenger from the brushmakers' district, out trying to find us.

RACHEL: A messenger?

[*A battered gnome emerges from the tunnel.*]

Shpunt!

SHPUNT: What then? You were expecting maybe the Prophet Isaiah? [*Rising painfully*] Climb up, climb down, crawl on your belly. What kind of life for a sick man?

RACHEL [*embraces him*]: It's really you. How on God's earth did you survive?

SHPUNT: On the way to the train I had a terrible fit. Palpitations. I fell on my face. Finished. The sergeant took a look at me. Thank God, even on a good day I look like a corpse. They left me lying there. I picked myself up and went into hiding.

KATZ: He tells us there is a party making up to leave by way of the sewers.

SHPUNT: They have a Pole, a repairman from the city waterworks, came to guide them out.

[*Crash of artillery fire.*]

MORDECAI: We haven't much time. They'll be starting any minute. They have a rendezvous on the other side—a certain manhole on Bonifratarska. Trucks are supposed to meet them there and take them to join the partisans.

[RUTKA *has crossed to pick up the baby.*]

RACHEL [*to* SHPUNT]: Are you going to lead us?

SHPUNT: What do you think I came all the way over here for, to borrow a handkerchief?

KATZ: We'll take nothing but weapons, and what's left of the water. [*To* SHPUNT] How far do we have to go in the open?

SHPUNT: Maybe thirty yards.

KATZ: We'll go one at a time. Ten-second intervals. Everyone ready?

[SHPUNT *exits into the tunnel.*]

Rutka . . . Mordecai.

[*They exit, followed by* RACHEL. BERSON *starts to go next, then pauses, and comes back into the bunker.*]

BERSON: Something's wrong.

[*One by one, those who have left tumble back.*]

KATZ: What is it?

SHPUNT: Germans. There must be fifty of them, coming this way.

[*Off, a sound of dogs baying.*]

MORDECAI: They spotted us. They'll be here in a minute, hunting for the entrance.

[*They are all frozen, listening to the dogs. Off, a burst of machine-gun fire.*]

[*The baby begins to cry.* RUTKA *rocks him desperately.*]

Do something! Get him quiet!

RUTKA: I'm trying!

[*Above the bunker, a* GERMAN SERGEANT *enters —pauses, listens, then whistles.*]

[*A* GERMAN PRIVATE *joins him. They both listen.*]

[*In the bunker,* KATZ *offers the vodka bottle, but* RUTKA *pushes it away.*]

RUTKA: It will only make him choke!

[MORDECAI *put his hand over the baby's mouth.* RUTKA *stands it as long as she can, then shoves his hand away.*]

He can't breathe!

[*The baby cries.*]

[*Above, the* GERMANS *gaze around, trying to gauge where the sound is coming from.*]

BERSON: Where's my concertina? [*He spies it, and grabs it.*]

RACHEL: Where are you going?

BERSON: To get them away from here.

RACHEL: No, Dolek, no, don't go out there!

[BERSON *pulls loose and exits. Trying to trace the*

sound, the GERMANS *move slowly off left.*]

[*The baby whimpers as* RUTKA *rocks him. Everyone listens tensely.*]

[*Outside the bunker,* BERSON *appears. He pauses for a moment, then begins to play* "Hatikvah" *on his concertina. Off, a burst of gunfire, close.* BERSON *breaks off, and crosses to exit, right.*]

RACHEL: Dolek!

[*From off, the concertina is heard again, playing a mocking rendition of* "Deutschland Uber Alles," *making it sound almost Yiddish. Off, a burst of machine-gun fire.*]

He's baiting them! He's leading them away!

[KATZ *has ducked into the tunnel.*]

[*From off, come the strains of Mendelssohn's* "Spring Song"—*a banal, satiric rendition. Further off in the distance, a shot is heard.*]

KATZ [*returning*]: The coast is clear. Now's our chance.

RACHEL: We have to wait for Dolek.

[KATZ *starts pushing* RUTKA *and* MORDECAI *into the tunnel.*]

SHPUNT: There is no time.

RACHEL: Please, wait, wait for him, he'll be back!

SHPUNT: And so will the Germans!

[SHPUNT *exits into the tunnel.* KATZ *comes to get* RACHEL.]

[*Somewhere off, the concertina is heard again, playing a Chopin Polonaise.*]

KATZ: Quickly.

RACHEL: No, no, wait! Wait for Dolek! [*Struggling with* KATZ] No . . . no . . . we have to wait for Dolek!

[*The sound of a shot is heard. The concertina music expires with a discordant moan.*]

RACHEL: Dolek . . .

[KATZ *wrestles her into the tunnel.*]

[*Above, one by one, the shadowy figures appear in the street.* RUTKA, MORDECAI, *and* SHPUNT *cross through the rubble, vanishing off right.* RACHEL *and* KATZ *appear.* RACHEL *gazes around desperately, as though hoping to find* BERSON *in the charred desolation.*]

RACHEL [*a despairing, whispered cry*]: Dolek . . .

[KATZ *shoves her on. She crosses right . . . hesitates in the ruins. Then* KATZ *catches up with her and takes her with him, off right.*]

[A *silence.*]

[*The concertina is heard again, echoing softly over the Ghetto, playing* "Dort'n, Dort'n"—*the indomitable song tenderly defying death.*]

CURTAIN

A NOTE ABOUT THE AUTHOR

MILLARD LAMPELL was born in Paterson, New Jersey, in 1919. After graduating from West Virginia University he worked as a process server, dye worker, coal miner, and folk singer. His celebrated cantata, *The Lonesome Train*, recounting the journey of Lincoln's funeral train, was first produced in 1945 and has subsequently been performed in eleven countries. He served as a sergeant in the United States Army Air Force from 1943 to 1946. His series of short war plays, *The Long Way Home*, was published in 1946. His novel, *The Hero*, was published in 1949 and was made into the film, *Saturday's Hero*, by Columbia Pictures. In 1959, *Journey to the Cape*, a book of poems and dialogues, was published.

January 1961